ONLY NUNS CHANGE
HABITS OVERNIGHT

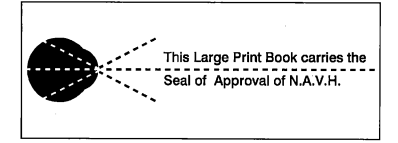

This Large Print Book carries the
Seal of Approval of N.A.V.H.

ONLY NUNS CHANGE HABITS OVERNIGHT

52 AMAZING WAYS TO MASTER THE ART OF PERSONAL CHANGE

KAREN LINAMEN

CHRISTIAN LARGE PRINT
A part of Gale, Cengage Learning

 GALE
CENGAGE Learning™

Detroit • New York • San Francisco • New Haven, Conn • Waterville, Maine • London

GALE
CENGAGE Learning

Details in some anecdotes and stories have been changed to protect the identities of the persons involved.

Christian Large Print Originals.

The text of this Large Print edition is unabridged.

Other aspects of the book may vary from the original edition.

Set in 16 pt. Plantin.

Printed on permanent paper.

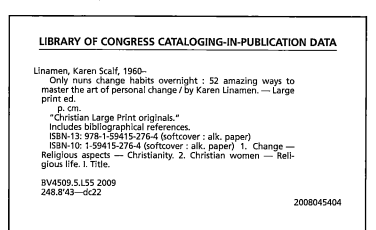

LIBRARY OF CONGRESS CATALOGING-IN-PUBLICATION DATA

Linamen, Karen Scalf, 1960–
    Only nuns change habits overnight : 52 amazing ways to
master the art of personal change / by Karen Linamen. — Large
print ed.
        p. cm.
    "Christian Large Print originals."
    Includes bibliographical references.
    ISBN-13: 978-1-59415-276-4 (softcover : alk. paper)
    ISBN-10: 1-59415-276-4 (softcover : alk. paper) 1. Change —
Religious aspects — Christianity. 2. Christian women — Religious life. I. Title.

    BV4509.5.L55 2009
    248.8'43—dc22

                                                    2008045404

Published in 2009 by arrangement with WaterBrook Press, a division of Random House, Inc.

Printed in the United States of America
1 2 3 4 5 6 7 12 11 10 09 08

*For my dad, R. Gene Scalf,
who has been teaching me
these principles ever since I was a toddler
sitting in his lap, listening
to Norman Vincent Peale, Napoleon Hill, and
others — on reel to reel! No one lives larger
or with greater optimism or
intention than this remarkable man.
This one's for you, Dad.*

CONTENTS

INTRODUCTION

PROMISES, PROMISES

So I'm standing in line at the supermarket the other day, and suddenly I spot something that gives me a surge of hope.

Right there, not two feet away, is a magazine cover promising me everything I've ever longed for. Imagine! For less than the price of a Venti Mocha Frappuccino, I can learn how to accomplish twice as much in half the time, get a bikini body in twenty-one days, discover sex-goddess secrets that are guaranteed to drive a man wild, abolish zits forever, protect myself from the hidden heart-attack risk even my doctor doesn't know about, and de-stress my life 147 different ways.

I feel better already.

On second thought . . . haven't I read these articles already? Except *last* month they promised I could learn how to multitask the *right* way, get the washboard abs I've always dreamed of, surprise my man with the sex move he secretly craves, look ten years younger, ask the health questions most women forget to ask, and streamline my chaotic life by next Tuesday.

Now that I think about it, I've been reading these same articles for years. So how come I'm still overworked, overstressed, ailment riddled, *and* look my age? You know as well as I that I'm not the only woman who longs to improve her life. You want the same things I do. And maybe, like me, there are things you've been struggling to change for years.

What's taking us so long?

I don't think our biggest problem is what we desire. Oh sure, sometimes we get our little hearts set on stuff that's kind of shallow, impractical, or even destructive. But I'm convinced that most of the time, you and I want healthy, sane things for ourselves and our families. So what's the problem? Why can't we take our longings — especially if the changes we want to make are wise and good — and consistently turn them into reality?

I believe one solution is to hone our "change skills." I'm convinced there are basic skills and techniques that, if we learn them well, can help us embrace the things we long for.

Okay, maybe not *everything*. Maybe not Jude Law. But if we truly master the change skills outlined in the pages of this book, we may be surprised to find that a lot of the stuff we've been longing for is within our reach after all.

I know a lot about longings. In fact, I wrote the book on longings. In *Chocolatherapy: Satisfying the Deepest Cravings of Your Inner Chick,* I talked about emotional eating and our cravings for chocolate and other binge favorites. But more specifically I talked about the things we're *really* hungry for. I examined twelve of our deepest cravings for things like love, community, answers, and even escape, then suggested calorie-free ways to satisfy these core longings.

I devoted my last book, *Due to Rising Energy Costs, the Light at the End of the Tunnel Has Been Turned Off,* to figuring out how to satisfy a single longing, which is the longing to experience happy, fabulous lives even when our circumstances look dim. I showed how you and I can stop letting our emotions be dictated by our circumstances and start experiencing peace, happiness, and hope — no matter what is happening around us.

But this book is *different.*

It's not about satisfying twelve core longings, or even how to turn your number-one longing into reality. This book is about learning fifty-two techniques that will empower you to pursue and embrace *any* change you long to make.

Oh sure, you and I will definitely chat about specific changes we'd love to embrace, like experiencing less fat on our bodies or more passion in our marriages or more hope in our hearts. But the longer I live, learn, and write about this stuff, the more I realize there are universal principles that apply to *any* kind of healthy, positive change that you and I yearn for.

1. Learn from the past.

Think about a few of your attempts during the past six months to make change happen. Did any of those efforts result in lasting change? If so, write down the factors that contributed to making change stick. If the change didn't last, try to determine what caused your attempts to fall short. Keep these things in mind as you read about the techniques of successful change in the chapters that follow.

✿

Wouldn't it be great if you and I really understood the principles of change? What if we had a good working knowledge of *how* to change, so that whenever anything came up that we wanted to tweak, we'd have a clue of what to do and how to begin?

Years ago, William Strunk Jr. wrote a little classic called *The Elements of Style.* Writers know that the collection of principles in Strunk's book apply to virtually every genre of writing and that, once we learn the principles, we've got the tools we need to attempt pretty much anything we want to write. Likewise, the book you hold in your hands contains fifty-two elements of change. Start learning these and putting them into practice and you'll be prepared to tackle almost any change you desire.

What *do* women want?

And more importantly, how do we get it?

You probably already know the answer to the first question, at least as far as it applies to you. In the following pages, you're going to discover the answer to the second question.

Yes, Virginia, it really *is* possible to craft a new chapter in your life, one in which transformations are within your reach and good things abound!

1

IS THERE SOMETHING THAT DOESN'T EXIST IN YOUR LIFE, BUT YOU WISH IT DID?

THE ART OF CHANGE

Last night I had dinner with four other women at Carino's Italian Grill. Since these were new acquaintances, I dressed up for the occasion, abandoning my fave black boots, jeans, and black jacket for an uncharacteristically neutral white tank, beige linen jacket, and — perfect for first impressions — these really great leopard pumps.

Across a table laden with bowls of lasagna, antipasto, and loaves of crusty bread, we introduced ourselves and began exchanging pleasantries. At first, we offered aerial shots of our worlds, like how many kids we had, how long we'd lived in Colorado, and the kinds of things that we or our husbands did for a living.

Gradually we began sharing snapshots of the landscapes of our lives, like when Becky told us about the week she spent bicycling through Europe with her husband and two teenage granddaughters.

But I wanted more. A closer glimpse. Call me Mrs. Kravitz if you must. But, like Darrin and Samantha's nosy neighbor, I longed for a peek inside the private quarters where these women lived. I told them I was writing a book on change and invited their insights. Then I asked if there were any changes in *their* lives they'd been longing to make.

I'll be the first to admit that, as questions go, "What kinds of changes have you been longing to make?" is onionesque, meaning the first layers are opaque and it takes a while to get down to the transparent stuff. The first round of responses was pretty much what any group of new acquaintances might offer. Nancy suggested there are seasons when a woman longs for change and other seasons when things are going great and she's happy with who she is and what she's got.

I leaned forward, careful to avoid the marinara sauce I'd managed to spill on the table beside my plate. (See why I always wear black?) I probed, "So, you're all pretty happy with your lives?"

There were nods all around the table.

I was intrigued. Most of these women were a little farther along the path of life than I was. Several had grandchildren the ages of my daughters. Is this what I had to look forward to? Somewhere in the next several years, would I find myself completely satisfied with my life? And if so, would it mean I'd finally learned how to create the changes I'd longed for? Or would it mean that I'd finally given up and let my desperate longings for change fall by the wayside? I wasn't too sure about all this.

About that time, Becky brought up her longing to relocate so she could be closer to kids and grandkids. She sighed. "I wish it could happen next month, but we've got to sell our property first, and it's not even listed yet. It could be a year before we finally get to move."

The conversation drifted then to real estate, children, and even gardening. After a while there was a lull, and Diane lit up and said, "Well, I'm starting school in the fall! That's a big change for me. In fact, I've wanted to do this for years!"

We plied her with questions: "If you've wanted to do this for years, what kept you from doing it sooner, and what made you decide to finally do it now?" "Will you attend classes part time or full time?" "How will you use all your new knowledge when you're done?"

2. Draw your own onion.

It's time for you to answer the onion question I posed to the women I met for dinner: "What changes have you been longing to make?" Just for fun, draw the face of an onion cut in half. It's easier than you might think: Draw a circle. Inside of that circle draw layers of concentric circles. Draw the circles closest to the outside edge a little farther apart (these are your thicker, tougher layers of onion). Draw the circles near the center a little closer together (these are your thinner, transparent layers of onion). Now ask yourself what changes you've been longing to make. Write your answers on your onion. Do any of your answers get to the heart of the matter? Do they represent the fragile, transparent stuff you really long for, the stuff you don't reveal to the world?

❈

Eventually someone said, "Well, as long as we're talking about changes, what woman doesn't wish she could lose a few pounds?" and we all groaned in wistful agreement.

One of the women made a face. "Why is it

so hard? I struggle and struggle. Look at you," and she tapped bicycling-through-Europe Becky playfully on the shoulder. "You don't have a problem with weight. Then again, I guess you work it off. But food calls my name. I wish we didn't have to eat at all. If someone wants to stop drinking, I hear they can take a pill that makes them sick to their stomach if they have a drink. Why can't we do that with food? Instead, we just have to eat *less.* I *hate* that!"

That started a humorous exchange of diet tips and stories.

As lighthearted conversation winged all around us, one of the women turned to just me and said quietly, "I long to change my perception of myself."

"You do?"

She nodded. "I'm too hard on myself. I know it. Even my husband says so."

She talked a little about being the firstborn in her family, being the daughter of a mother she'd never been able to please, feeling bound by the need to be not only perfectly perfect but perfectly nice as well, and chastising herself when she fell short of these impossible goals.

Toward the end of our evening at Carino's, one of the women looked at me and asked, "So what changes do *you* want to make?"

I only gave her the short list, mentioning my desires to . . .

- Become better organized with my finances.
- Settle into a committed, long-term relationship with my skinny jeans (replacing all these short-lived flings).
- Fall madly in love.
- Launch an idea I have for a community-wide monthly event called Second Saturday in the Springs. The idea came to me when I was sifting through the ashes of a loss in my life. Who knows? Maybe it's my phoenix. All I know is that I can't seem to get this idea out of my head, so I'm thinking it's time to rearrange my life to make it happen.

I forgot to mention that I'd love to be a neater eater so I could feel more confident wearing something other than black.

3. Revisit those ashes.
Undoubtedly you've had times in your life when something has crashed and burned. Maybe it was a dream you were pursuing. Or a relationship you valued. Or maybe

even your own hope, happiness, and joy as you experienced a season of burnout or even depression. Think back on those times. Revisit those ashes. Kick around in the rubble a little. What gems are hiding there? Is there a tenacious flower that has taken root despite the loss — and it's growing stubbornly up through the debris, waiting to be transplanted to more fertile ground?

Sometimes the ashes and rubble of our worst experiences yield unexpected treasure. Take a few minutes to make a list of some of the darkest experiences in your life. Now write down any longings, new visions, goals, convictions, or desires that came from those experiences. Some dreams need to die, to be sure. Some deserve to be resurrected. Others, in their death, give birth to new and different longings. The truth is that endings and beginnings are one and the same. I know you've experienced endings in your life. The question remains: what new beginnings are waiting to be pursued?

As the evening drew to a close, we paid our tabs and went our separate ways. Driving home, two things occurred to me.

The first was that, sadly, I had a big glob of marinara sauce on my linen jacket.

The second was that it had been an intriguing evening.

THE CHANGE'LL DO YOU GOOD

What changes do you long to embrace? It's an onion of a question, to be sure. But as you peel away the layers, isn't it *fascinating*?

Some changes come immediately to mind and tongue. Other transformations feel so unattainable that we barely admit our longings to ourselves, much less to other people.

Truth is, I haven't met a woman who doesn't have something in her life she longs to change. It might be the clutter in her home or the frown on her lips, the shape of her nose or the size of her hips, the balance in her checkbook, the crack in her heart. Perhaps she's convinced that her ring finger needs a golden band or her marriage needs a spark. She might long to trade chaos for calm, bitterness for freedom, or that pack of Virginia Slims for a breath of fresh air. It's possible that she yearns to exchange her plus-size polyester for a pair of size-nine jeans. Maybe she longs for a better career.

Or a second chance. Or a dream she can feel passionate about.

What kinds of changes do we long to embrace? The list is endless. We want greater connection with loved ones, the fulfillment of long-held dreams, beautiful bodies, freedom from the hurts and beliefs that keep us from living the lives we desire. We want healthy, committed, happy, passionate marriages. We long for greater control in our finances and greater abandon in our hearts.

So what's stopping us? Why do we stay stuck in the same ruts year after year?

The Art of Change

I don't know what changes you've been longing to embrace. But no matter what changes you dream of, there are principles you can use to create those changes. I've thought about the best way to characterize the principles that produce change. Actually, the word *principles* would be fine if it didn't make me think of textbooks. There's got to be a better word.

Tools? Too much testosterone.

Strategies? Sounds like a military campaign.

Tips? Mmm . . . seems wishy-washy to me.

How 'bout *pillars,* as in "the pillars of change"? It sounds established, doesn't it?

Kind of like an ancient Greek temple or maybe the president of the local Rotary (you know, pillar of the community and all that). But I'm the kind of girl who writes notes to herself using lip liner and thinks carrot cake should count as a vegetable, so *pillars* seems a bit staid for me.

~~Ahhh . . . I know~~ *exactly* ~~what to call these~~ principles of change: *media.* No, not like *WKRP in Cincinnati.* Not that kind of media. I mean media as in *art.*

Media is what an artist uses to create beauty. She begins with an image in her mind, a picture or vision of something that doesn't exist, but should. Then she chooses her medium. Watercolor? Acrylics? Skin and pigment? Stone and chisel? How 'bout silver sequins, wooden beads, uncooked spaghetti, Elmer's glue, and a box of empty toilet paper rolls? She's also got to understand techniques, like shading and perspective, and maybe even how to wield a can of spray paint. If she's sculpting, she'll need to understand balance and leverage. If she's tattooing or welding, different techniques will come into play.

Bottom line, if she's going to bring her vision to life, she's going to need *media,* which is a combination of raw materials, and knowledge. It might sound like a lot of work, gathering all that stuff and know-how. And sometimes the process can feel a little messy and random — but it is *so* worth the effort. After all, even a baby knows the joys of creating art out of whatever raw materials she has available to her. Just ask the toddler who is busy finger painting the wall next to her crib with whatever organic substance she had on hand . . . or bottom.

That's pretty much what this book is about. It's about taking the really cool picture that you envision in your head and creating it as a real thing in your life.

It's about the art of change.

---

4. Don't despise small changes.
Even a really small change can lead to bigger and better things. You've seen it happen with decorating. You buy a new pillow, and suddenly the couch seems shabby in comparison. You replace the couch and realize the colors in the rug don't match. You buy a different rug, and suddenly the armchair seems all wrong, and before you know it you're looking at paint chips.

In the same way, a single healthy change — like a stone tossed into a pond — can

---

create ripples of positive change throughout your entire life! For example, did you know that simply sleeping ninety minutes more each night — cranking up your shuteye from five and a half hours to seven — can not only improve your attitude, it can also decrease your appetite and lower your chances of suffering a heart attack?[1] Identify one single, small change that could create ripples of positive change in your life.

✻

Somewhere in your head are wistful images of a more satisfying life, sexier body, more secure future, happier heart, more intimate relationships, more defined purpose, or a lasting impact you want to make. In the pages of this book you'll find the media you need to create the art of change in your life. Believe it or not, you *can* begin to fashion the thing you see — starting now.

While it's true that only nuns change habits overnight, you *can* bring about the change you long for. And it doesn't need to happen overnight. You can learn how to become an artist of change, getting familiar with a variety of materials and techniques you can use to beautify your life. And, as you and I practice this new art, maybe we'll actually become talented at this creative thing called transformation.

Are you ready to embrace some of the changes you've been longing to make? Me too. Even if we don't get it right the first time. Even if it takes a little practice. Even if the process takes a few unexpected turns and we find ourselves in need of a little help along the way.

Speaking of which, does anyone know how to get spaghetti sauce off a linen jacket?

The Art of Change

Questions for personal reflection or group discussion:

How common is the longing for change? Do you know any people who are perfectly content with their lives? What are some of the more common things that people long to change?

Is contentment a lost art? How do we strike a healthy balance between contentment and change?

29

How can we know which one to strive for in any given situation? What would you love to change in your life? Are you answering from the opaque surface of the onion or from the transparent core? If you could peel away all your protective layers and answer this question in the most candid way you know how, would your answers change? Why are you reading this book (or why did you join this group), and how do you hope to benefit by doing so?

2

THE BAD NEWS IS THAT YOU'RE DISSATISFIED. THE GOOD NEWS IS THAT YOU'RE DISSATISFIED.

WHAT IF THE HOKEY POKEY REALLY *IS* WHAT IT'S ALL ABOUT?

My twelve-year-old was dissatisfied with her room. She told me, "There's something missing."

I had to agree. We had lived in this house for nearly a year, and all we'd managed to do in Kacie's room was paint the walls a bright shade of turquoise. *Three* shades of turquoise, to be exact. The bottom third of each wall sported the darkest color. The middle third was a lighter shade. The top third and ceiling had been painted the lightest shade of all. The goal had been to make her room look like it was under water. Instead, it just looked . . . well, *really* turquoise.

We were sitting on her bed when Kacie voiced her dissatisfaction. I looked around the room and had to agree with her. "Let's brainstorm," I said. And then we sat there for more than an hour, lobbing ideas back and forth.

One of us said, "We could paint fish on the walls."

"Or we could buy big wallpaper fish and stick 'em up there."

"We need something on the ceiling."

"Could we put some seaweed up there? Like it's floating?"

"No, wait! A boat. We could paint part of the ceiling so it looks like the bottom of a boat."

"What if we dropped a fishing line from the boat? With a hook on the end? Okay, a fake hook."

"Plus we could put something around the bed . . ."

"Like what? Plywood? Fabric?"

"We need a cave. Made of plywood. How 'bout an underwater sea cave!"

"A cave?"

"Yes! Can't you see it? It could start here, go up to there, and end over here . . . and the mouth of it would go from here to here. We could even drape shimmery blue fabric across the opening."

You can see a picture of our cave at www .karenlinamen.com. The good news is that Kacie *loves* her bedroom, and I have to admit it turned out even better than we imagined. Hard to believe what you can do with a couple sheets of plywood and some spray paint. Although, if you ask me, the plywood wasn't the most important part. I think the really important elements of our masterpiece came first, before the wood, before the paint and screws.

It all started with the words, "There's something missing."

IS THIS AS GOOD AS IT GETS?

I don't enjoy discontent. Neither am I fond of rope burns, electrolysis, or tax audits. In fact, discomfort in any area of my life makes me wince. Unfortunately, more often than not, discomfort is the first ingredient of change.

Well, all right, not *every* change is fueled by discomfort. Changes in our *external circumstances* don't need discomfort or pain to get them rolling. In fact, you and I both know what it feels like to be cruising along, happy and comfortable, when something happens — an accident, a reversal of fortune, an unwanted diagnosis, a pink slip — that changes everything. Yep, when it comes to external circumstances, change can occur in a heartbeat, even when we're at our happiest.

But when it comes to *internal* transformation — transformations that require or produce stuff like courage, growth, reconciliation, wisdom — discomfort isn't optional.

It's mandatory.

What is the stuff that is making *you* uncomfortable and discontented, or causing pain in your life? Are you secretly traumatized by that extra sixty pounds you wear? Do you wake up every morning dreading another day in the same house with the man whose wedding ring you wear? Does the meager paycheck from your dead-end job leave you feeling squeezed in ways only a cantaloupe could appreciate? Are you discouraged by the dearth of genuine relationships in your life? Do you look around at your very blue world and think, *There's something missing?*

Then take heart. You possess the first and most important element for change. Stop thinking of your discontent, dissatisfaction, or pain as a dead end, and start thinking of it as a doorway. If you've given birth, you know that labor pains open the doorway for new life to emerge. Emotional discomfort can do the same thing, paving the way for the miracles of transformation, growth, and new beginnings.

In other words, your dissatisfaction can serve you well, so take good care of it. Don't drown it in alcohol, bury it with food, or try to distract yourself with an affair. And for crying out loud, don't wallow in it either. Dissatisfaction is a tool. Would a carpenter lie down and roll around in his tools? (If he did, it certainly wouldn't make a very *level* bed. *Ba-da-BUM.*)

---

5. Make a list of your doorways.
It helps to list the stuff that is causing discontent — even pain — in your life. You've been seeing those things as problems, right? Making a list will help you change your perspective. Go ahead and list all the stuff that's been driving you nuts.

Now, close your eyes and picture these problems or losses as doorways to change, transformation, and growth. Open your eyes and check your list again. Can you see anything on that list in a new light? (If not, close your eyes again and try it one more time . . .)

My point is, don't waste your dissatisfaction. Wield it.

But dissatisfaction is only the beginning. You need something else before transformation has a fighting chance.

Can You See It?

A few weeks after my conversation with Kacie, I picked up the phone and called Jieils, a twenty-something-year-old craftsman my daughters and I found last year on Craigslist.org, a classifieds Web site. We hired him to install laminate in a hallway, then adopted him as a friend of the family.

I said, "Jieils, can you build a sea cave?"

He said, "You bet I can."

Kacie, her friend Lexi, my niece Gabriella, and I spray-painted the plywood to make it look like piles of stones, and Jieils took it from there. But even before we made the very first trip to Home Depot for supplies, the sea cave already existed in Kacie's mind and mine. And that image became our blueprint. It was the map from here to there. It became the bridge we needed to cross over from living in discontent to . . . well, sleeping in a sea cave.

Do you wish something in your life were different? Are you wondering how to get from here to there? It's one thing to realize that, at this very moment, something in your life happens to be amiss. It's another thing altogether to wake up next week to a life that is transformed and fulfilling.

What's in the middle? I can tell you exactly

what's in the middle: between dissatisfaction and transformation is *vision.*

Before we can create something in our worlds, we need to craft it in our heads. As Vincent van Gogh wrote about his masterpieces, "The thing has already taken form in my mind before I start on it."[1] It's true for paintings, and it's true for our lives as well. If we *see* it, there's a good chance we can figure out how to *do* it.

Henry David Thoreau described it this way: "You have built castles in the air . . . Now put the foundations under them."[2] What an amazing image! Imagine an elaborate castle hovering weightlessly above you. Perhaps it's twenty feet in the air, or maybe thirty or even fifty. Whatever the distance, it is unreachable and uninhabitable. Now imagine yourself grabbing hold of trowel and brick and mortar — solid, tangible elements from your very real world — and getting to work. You begin stacking and shaping, building brick by brick, higher and higher toward your dream castle. At times, hefting all those rough-hewn bricks is harder than you ever imagined. But then you fall into a rhythm of sorts, which evolves into a kind of momentum, and eventually — at the risk of sounding crazy — you'd swear some of the bricks have taken on lives of their own, moving effortlessly into place as if the castle hovering above you had some sort of gravitational pull, the way the moon pulls at the ocean.

And before you know it, that castle isn't hovering anymore. It's not out of reach, because you've altered the landscape of your world until the castle is sitting right in front of you. Now go on. Lower the drawbridge and saunter on in. Because that castle isn't in the air anymore. It's where you live.

A Fractured Fairy Tale

I was a weird kid. But even as a kid, I had something going for me. I had built a castle in the air. I was a toothless six-year-old, and people would smile at me and say, "What do you want to be when you grow up, little girl?" I never hesitated. Never even blinked. Instead, I'd announce with gusto, "I'm going to be a *writer!*"

Every chance I got, I stacked a single brick in the empty space beneath my floating castle. What kinds of bricks? I read books constantly (each one a brick) and wrote short stories and poetry (more bricks). When I was twelve, I rallied my two sisters and several friends and published a neighborhood magazine (another brick). When I was fourteen, my mom gave me a subscription to *Writer's Digest,* yet another brick in the foundation I

38

was laying. I wrote for school newspapers and worked on yearbooks. In college, I majored in journalism (still more bricks), attended my first writers' conference (a brick), and completed my first book-length manuscript (yep, another brick).

The summer before my senior year at Biola University, the annual trade show that is attended by every Christian book publisher and representatives of most Christian bookstores was held in Anaheim, California, a mere twenty minutes from my house. When one of my professors finagled me a badge to get into the convention center, I couldn't have been more thrilled! What an amazing opportunity to find a publisher for my book! Ecstatic, I stayed up all night preparing sample chapters of a manuscript I'd been working on for months.

The next morning, standing in the foyer of the Anaheim Convention Center, I was as scared and excited as I'd ever been. This was it. The moment I'd been working toward for my entire life. My shoulder ached beneath the strap of the canvas bag into which I'd loaded dozens of copies of my manuscript. I envisioned hundreds of editors milling about the exhibit hall, all of them anxious to get their hands on copies of my masterpiece, which I was prepared to dole out like candy in a schoolyard.

But as the day wore on and I walked the endless aisles between publishers' exhibits, nothing was as I'd imagined. Men and women milled about, sure, but no one looked the least bit like an editor. What's worse, they all seemed to know one another, greeting each other and laughing and talking shop while I felt invisible. I wandered, unseen, until late afternoon.

My shoulders throbbed. My back ached. My feet sprouted blisters the size of small farm animals. My brain felt fuzzy because I had stayed up all night preparing manuscripts. But it was my hope that took the worst beating of all. In seven hours on the convention floor, I hadn't spoken to a soul. Every manuscript I'd lugged into that hall was still in my canvas bag, except — unlike me — my manuscripts must have made a few friends during the day and invited them home with us, because my bag seemed to weigh ten times what it had that morning.

I'd never been so discouraged in my life.

Plodding back to my car, I pictured a huge wall of glass. It had felt like I was on the wrong side of the glass, watching a world I couldn't touch, a world I was desperate to be part of. I still wanted to get to the other side even though I had no idea how. Seems the

40

only thing I knew for sure was that I wasn't going to get there that day. But there had to be a way, there just *had* to . . .

But right then, the thing I needed most was sleep. And probably some chocolate. But I knew that after some shuteye and a five-pound bag of M&M's, I'd unpack all my thoughts again and see what I could figure out.

---

6. Lay a brick today.

This is without a doubt the best time to get started. Remember, before you can create something in your world, you need to craft it in your head.

a. Describe a few of your castles in the air.

b. Now write down ten things you can do that would stack ten bricks in the foundation. This is the foundation that, once completed, could make your castle a dream come true.

c. Out of the ten things you listed, circle one thing you can do today.

d. Do it.

☀

I was twenty-two when I attended that publishing trade show. It would be five years before I'd return. But when I did return, I had my own publisher, a book to promote, and a handful of people who knew me by name.

A few years after my first book was published, I was cruising the exhibit hall, meeting with editors and greeting friends and colleagues at every turn, when I was stopped in my tracks by a startlingly clear memory of that first lonely convention. But it wasn't a painful thought at all. It was a really cool reminder of how you don't have to stay outside, peering longingly through a glass wall. Indeed, if you hang on to your vision and keep shaping your life — brick by brick — toward your dream, you can get where you want to be.

So keep building castles in the sky. The shadows they cast on the ground will show you where to stack your bricks. And before you know it, you'll be home, sweet home.

HAVE YOU EVER SEEN A RABBIT WEARING GLASSES?

Do you have a clear picture of what you want your life to look like in the near future? If not, are you ready to improve your vision? Carrots might keep Peter Cottontail out of bifocals, but you and I are going to need something stronger than taproots if we want a clear view of a brighter future.

Here are three ideas.

Start a dream journal

In *The Rhythm of Life,* Matthew Kelly explains what he does to give himself plenty to look toward in the future. He keeps a journal and fills it with no-holds-barred, wild-eyed whims and heartfelt desires. He writes:

> My dream-book is filled with pages and pages of dreams . . . Everything from countries I'd like to visit, books I'd like to write, and the qualities I'd like my soulmate to have, to living by the beach, driving a sweet little convertible, cycling down Haleakala at sunrise, and virtues I'd like to develop in my own character.[3]

Start your own dream-book. Write. Doodle. Clip pictures from magazines and paste them in the pages of your book. Every one of these is a blueprint. You may or may not choose to take every blueprint and build it in your life, but it's nice to know you could try if you wanted to!

7. Keep your dreams in front of you.

What do you want your life to look like in ten years? Ten weeks? How about tomorrow? What experiences would you like to have before you die? Are there exotic places you'd love to visit? Think big, small, or out of the box. Make lists, doodle, or paste clippings from newspapers or magazines into a journal, glue them onto a big sheet of poster board, or tack them onto a bulletin board. Just get started!

☀

Don't limit what you "see" to just the stuff that "makes sense"

Kids are experts at this one. Ask any kid what she wants to be when she grows up, and she'll tell you. The best part is that her answer could range from schoolteacher to Navy SEAL. And it doesn't matter if the dream she describes never comes true. The act of dreaming big dreams — regardless of how they turn out — leaves us expanded and richer as a result.

Kids not only see future stuff more readily than we do, they also have 20/20 vision when it comes to seeing imaginary stuff. I'll never

44

forget the day I checked my rearview mirror while driving down a Texas freeway. Framed in the mirror was my three-year-old, strapped in her car seat with tears rolling down her cheeks.

"Kacie! What's wrong!"

She said sorrowfully, "Tito bit me!"

Tito was her imaginary dog.

See what I mean?

8. Color outside the lines.

Picture something you've always told yourself you shouldn't do. Now ask yourself, Why not? If you can't think of a single reason not to do it, then go out and do it. (And *please* tell me I don't need to insert disclaimers here that include words like *illegal* or *dangerous*.)

Need ideas? Eat dessert before dinner. Play music way too loud. Turn on every light in the house. Sleep till noon. Wear something daring. Go to the theater and pay to watch two movies in a row (oh, you wild woman, you!).

When you're dreaming, don't limit yourself. Every now and then my daughters and

I grab crayons and coloring books, plop on our stomachs on the floor, and go to town. I usually color inside the lines, but I *never* make everything the color it's "supposed" to be. On my pages, apples are purple, clouds are teal, and penguins wear polka dots.

When my kids were little, they would point at my pictures and scoff, saying, "You can't do that!"

I'd always ask, "Why not?"

They could never give me a good answer.

As you're dreaming big dreams, ask yourself the same question: Why not? We all know that not every wild whim is a good idea. But when you're dreaming up something new, why not start with the far-fetched — you never know what will become reality!

So if there are no valid reasons *not* to, go for it! Let your imagination soar, right up there with that polka-dotted penguin flying through teal clouds.

Expose yourself regularly to new thoughts and ideas

Every now and then I read a book, watch a movie, or attend a performance or event that is so awe-inspiring I'm overcome with an ache. It's visceral, and it's part yearning, part regret, part inspiration. I yearn for the bittersweet experience of creating something even half as beautiful as what I've just seen and heard; I'm filled with regret that I have yet to scratch the surface of the vast creative potential that's in every one of us; and I'm inspired to do a better job of exploring and developing my own creativity in the future. Glimpsing what's *possible,* I become less satisfied with what *is.*

As we find ourselves exposed to exceptional things — ideas, creative genius, beauty, discipline, talent, examples of selflessness — we not only increase our awareness of what's possible in our own lives, we can also increase our discontent. But as we have seen, that may not be such a bad thing.

---

9. Inspire yourself.

What inspires you to reach higher and to dream bigger? Is it the creative triumph of the performing arts? the adrenaline and do-or-die human drama at a sporting event? the quiet brilliance of a great book? Make a short list of things that fill you with awe and remind you of the magic and potential of life.

This week, expose yourself to one of the things on your list.

☀

Read books. Attend plays. Browse art galleries. Take a class. Watch underdog-saves-the-day movies that leave you inspired and motivated. Surround yourself with excellence. Stay on the lookout for examples of people who attained dreamed-of potential. Pay attention to the stories of women and men who have imagined and then accomplished something they longed to do.

You'll gain a deeper understanding of the world around you. But more importantly, you'll gain a deeper understanding of the world *within* you. You want to know what's possible? You want to know what you can do? Then read, watch, listen, learn, and grow. As you do, your dreams and visions for your life will soar to a whole new level.

Unless your name is Ariel, you've probably never felt the need to sleep in a sea cave. That's okay. Whatever it is you're longing for, don't let your discontent scare you. You're not stuck. You haven't reached a dead end. If you know how to use it, your discontent can be a doorway, your pain a portal.

And vision is your key.

The Art of Change

Questions for personal reflection or group discussion:

Whether you're by yourself or in a group, before you answer the questions below, first do this exercise:

a. Close your eyes, and visualize one of the changes you long for — and be specific. Imagine six very specific details about the change you'd love to see in your life. For example, don't say, "I'd like to lose weight." Close your eyes, and imagine the completed change. Tell me what you're wearing, how free your movements are, what your emotions are after you have lost the desired amount of weight. Details! Details!

b. Keeping your eyes closed, spend three minutes developing and practicing that image in your mind. Three minutes. Time it. *(Tick tock tick tock tick tock.)*

All done? How did that feel? Take a few minutes to journal (if you're by yourself) or discuss (if you're with a group) the detailed image you just created and enjoyed. Will you commit to spending three minutes a day for the next thirty days reimagining this vision in your mind?

Do you agree that it's important to picture in your mind the change you want to make? Why or why not? What benefits might you enjoy by using your imagination to "see" the end result you desire?

Can you think of examples from Scripture that support the idea that what you create in your thoughts (whether positive or negative) is very likely to be created in your life? As you think about this, read Luke 6:45; Proverbs 23:7 (KJV); Proverbs 29:18 (KJV); and Philippians 4:8.

3

HOW LONG DOES IT TAKE TO CHANGE YOUR LIFE?

DECIDE AND CONQUER

I was a preemie baby, born seven weeks before my due date. That's the last time I've arrived anywhere early. That is why, a few months after moving with her family from Washington State to a home in my Colorado neighborhood, my sister Renee smiled at me and said, "Thank you."

I said, "For what?"

She said, "My kids used to give me a hard time about being late. Now they're grateful. They say I'm not late at all compared to Aunt Karen."

The bad news is that I'm always late. The good news is that my tardiness sets a low benchmark that makes other moms look great.

I may have figured out what my problem is. My problem is that I don't live in a nudist colony. If I did, I would never be late because my most pressing decision every morning would be whether to wear the coconut-scented sunscreen or the fragrance free. There would be no need to try on seven different outfits before walking out the door — which is what I do most mornings.

I don't know why getting dressed is such an ordeal. Sometimes I try to get an earlier start by simply wearing what I wore the day before. I'll admit my weight fluctuates a lot, but if something fit on Wednesday, the odds are decent it'll still fit on Thursday. Sounds simple, doesn't it?

That's what I used to think too. At least until my six-year-old niece, Gabriella, spent the night at my house and observed me getting dressed the next morning.

"You wore those jeans yesterday," she announced.

"Yep."

"And that shirt."

"I know."

"At least wear a different belt."

I happen to know something Gabriella doesn't know, which is that, in my world, switching belts requires numerous try-ons, several rounds of evaluations, and maybe even a nominating convention. At that moment I didn't have the time. I needed to be somewhere by Tuesday.

I shook my head. "Thanks, sweetie, that's a

nice idea, but I think I'll wear the same belt."

Determined, Gabriella said, "I'll give you ten points for anything you wear that you didn't wear yesterday."

I perked up. "Ten points? Really?" Between bra and panties, I figured I'd already earned twenty. Maybe thirty if I could convince her that underwear should get double points because they're called a "pair." But before I worked too hard at this, I needed to know what was at stake. I folded my arms. "So what exactly can I do with all these points?"

She looked blank. "Do with them?"

"If I earn a bunch of points, what do I get? Do I get a second helping of dessert? half an hour longer before bedtime? a manicure or maybe a Gucci bag?"

She shrugged. "I don't know. They're just points. I guess you can decide to do whatever you want with them."

"I have to *decide?*"

"Yep."

I started rummaging through the hamper. She said, "What are you doing?"

"Looking for yesterday's underclothes."

"Why are you doing that?"

"I can't afford any points! If I have to make one more decision, there's a good chance I won't get out of the house until spring!"

53

FAILED RESOLUTIONS . . . NOT JUST FOR NEW YEAR'S ANYMORE!

I'm not always indecisive. Sometimes I make ironclad decisions that have the lifespan of a mayfly. (For non-mayfly-enthusiasts, that's about four hours.)

Diets tend to fall into this category. I've found that I can adhere to pretty much any diet, no matter how restrictive, in the four hours between lunch and dinner. After that, anything goes.

The problem is that I'm easily distracted. A couple weeks ago a friend and I were chatting in my living room when he said, "Karen, you're the kind of person who can be in the middle of something and suddenly go, 'Oh look! There's a monkey!' and you're off and running in another direction."

What's funny is that when he said that, I *did* look.

There was no monkey, but Steve has a good point. All this distractibility means life never gets boring. But it also means that creating lasting change can be challenging.

10. Make it official.

Stop waffling. Go ahead and identify a change you long to embrace! Now, decide

54

to change it. And this time, make a real decision. Did you decide to pursue the change you want to make, or are you still just toying with the idea? It's time to stop playing around. Make the decision *now*, or at least before you fall asleep tonight.

※

What about you? How are you at making decisions . . . and sticking to them?

Let's admit it. If vacillating, daydreaming, hesitation, and diversion were effective ways to achieve our deepest desires, you and I would be size-six, Pulitzer Prize–winning, billionaire, fashion-magazine cover girls by now.

But we're not. So maybe it's time for a new strategy.

HOW LONG DOES IT TAKE TO CHANGE YOUR LIFE?

You've probably heard some experts say it takes twenty-one days to change a habit. Others believe change can require a lifetime.

But here's the truth: you can change your life much sooner. In fact, you can change your life in a heartbeat, which is how long it can take to make a single decision.

You don't believe you can change your life in a heartbeat? I've already confessed that decision making is not my forte. And yet, even in my chronically commitment-phobic existence, there have been times when my entire life has pivoted on a single decision.

I remember one of the really big heartbeats. I was a college freshman listening to a chapel speaker at Biola University when I made the life-changing decision to stop saying, "I hope I can be a writer one day," and start saying, "I *am* a writer."

I remember another heartbeat. I was at Miceli's Italian Restaurant in Hollywood, California, sitting across the table from a man who had proposed to me two months earlier. That's when I made the life-changing decision to say yes to marriage.

11. Make *one* ironclad decision today.
Flex your decision-making muscles. Your decision can be as sane as "I'm actually going to drink those eight glasses of water everybody's always harping about" or as silly as "every hour on the hour I'm going to sing the opening stanza of 'My Sharona' or 'Hotel California.'" Make it something doable, then do it. When you're getting

started, what you choose isn't as important as getting used to the victory feeling
that comes with getting it done.

✺

I remember the heartbeat just after I
caught a glimpse of myself in a store mirror
— when I made the life-extending decision
to lose sixty pounds and reclaim my body
and my health.

I remember a middle-of-the-night heartbeat. Feeling tormented over chaos and pain
in my life, I'd gone for a long walk at one in
the morning and was standing on a starlit
street several miles from my house. At that
moment, I made the eternity-altering decision to believe in God whether or not I'd
"felt" His presence lately in my bruised and
hurting life.

I remember the heartbeat when my life
changed while I was standing in front of an
unscrupulous ice-cream truck driver. He
had just cheated my kids out of the change
from their hard-earned dollar bills, and I de-
bated whether to make a scene over sixteen
cents. That's when I made the pivotal decision to stop trying to avoid confrontation at
any cost and start standing up for what I

knew to be true.

In these instances and others, I made a single decision, and my life changed as a result. Sure, some of the changes — like losing sixty pounds or making the journey from wannabe to writer to published writer — took months or even years to fully achieve. But that doesn't alter the fact that by making a single decision — and sticking with it — even a decision-challenged invertebrate like myself can realize profound and sometimes even immediate results.

We can spend days or even years pining, whining, or craving. We can wish, regret, or daydream. We can wistfully ponder, ruefully wonder, or even longingly hanker.

Or we can make a decision and take an action.

How long will it take to change your life?

You tell me.

PRACTICE MAKES PERFECT

If, like me, you have underdeveloped muscles when it comes to making decisions and sticking to them, you'll be thrilled to know that a little practice really can yield great results. As you and I learn how to make and execute small decisions quickly and thoroughly, just think what we can do with big, important decisions!

58

The bad news is that there are countless little decisions you and I try to make every day that trip us up. The good news is that these are great opportunities for practice and growth. So how can we start to exercise our decision-making and follow-through muscles?

Here's an example: what if I trained myself to look at a menu and make a healthy decision quickly instead of dawdling and second-guessing every menu choice until the waitress starts looking around for a bus to step in front of?

12. Turn an idea into a decision.

If it's in your head, you have an idea. Put that idea on paper and you have a goal. Make it measurable and you have a strategy. Put a deadline to it and you have a decision.

"I'm going to get control of my finances." Good idea. "I'm going to reduce mindless spending by fifty dollars every week for the next six weeks." Now that's a decision.

a. What's your good idea?

b. Phrase it in a way that makes it measurable.

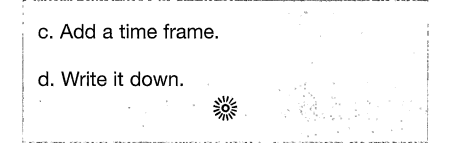
What if I learned how to open my bedroom closet, make a quick selection, dress quickly, and hang up any leftover pieces of clothing that might be lying around the room? Every single morning?

What if, the next time I bring in my mail, I actually completed the task, tossing junk mail, filing important papers, and paying bills rather than letting the growing stack dawdle on my kitchen counter for days?

What if, the next time I decide to lose ten pounds, I really did it?

What if you and I took the whole thing a step further, making up small, attainable goals just so we could practice the art of turning a goal into reality? What if we made the decision to give up coffee for three days? Or stick with a vegetarian diet for twenty-four hours? Or walk around the block every morning for a week? Or spend thirty minutes a day for an entire month playing the piano?

What if we decided to turn off the television for an entire weekend?

Or attend church every week for a month?

Or do one random act of kindness every day for two weeks?

Pretty soon, all these smaller victories will give us greater confidence, stamina, and experience. Then when we attempt the bigger decisions — to save a marriage, cut up our

13. Tell a cheerleader.

Chances are, you have a few friends who are cheerleaders. (I'm certain you also have friends who could find something to criticize about Mom's apple pie, Lassie, or winning a million dollars!) Choose a few friends or family members from group A, who are by nature positive and encouraging "can-do" folks who understand the power of an encouraging word.

Now, tell these cheerleaders about a decision you've made that will have a positive impact on your life. Are they excited for you? Do they believe you can do this? Let their encouragement and enthusiasm inspire you to push ahead toward achieving your goal!

charge cards, master a musical instrument, get back in shape, change careers, get over our anger, reclaim our joy, or get out of debt — we've got muscle. We know exactly what it feels like to make healthy decisions and follow them through to completion. We've been practicing.

We can do it.

THE CURE FOR THE COMMON RUT

Are you suffering from indecision? short-lived resolutions? unrealized goals? If so, these maladies are probably keeping you from embracing the changes you've been longing to make.

How can you spell relief?

M-A-K-E-a-D-E-C-I-S-I-O-N-a-n-d-F-O-L-L-O-W-i-t- T-H-R-O-U-G-H.

Sure, it has a lot of letters, but with a little practice it's not such a big pill to swallow. Plus, as far as remedies go, there are no unpleasant side effects. With consistent application, you'll enjoy newfound freedom as you not only set the goals you want but make them come true. Imagine! The power to reinvent your life will finally be within your grasp!

And as a special incentive, if you place your order today, we'll throw in an all-expense-paid, week-long vacation to an exotic tropical location. Once you are no longer bothered by indecision, short-lived resolutions, and unrealized goals, you'll enjoy this opportunity to relax among new friends. Best of all, you can be confident that, since discovering the cure for the common rut, you'll be prepared to handle whatever decisions you might have to make.

Although, considering where we're sending you, your most pressing decision will be pretty simple: should you wear the coconut-scented sunscreen or the fragrance-free?

The Art of Change

Questions for personal reflection or group discussion:

On a scale of one to ten, how effective are you at making good decisions and sticking to them? Why did you rate yourself as you did?

Do you find yourself making the same decision over and over again because you can't seem to follow it through to completion? Name one of your leading "repeat decisions."

When you make a decision and don't follow through, how does it affect your life? How have failed resolutions impacted your emotions or beliefs, hope, and confidence? How could they affect your future behavior? your relationships with other people? your feelings about yourself? your relationship with God?

Take a few minutes to identify the leading reasons why you're having a hard time making a decision and following through with it. Are you unsure about this decision, or are you confident it's something you *really* want to do? Are you biting off more than you can chew? If so, in what way? Are outside factors hindering you? If outside obstacles are a problem, what can you do about them?

Would moving to a nudist colony solve any challenges or problems in your life — such as relieving you of daily, time-consuming decisions? Why or why not?

4

SOMETIMES A GIRL NEEDS A LITTLE SOMETHING TO GET HER GOING.

INSTANT HUMAN. JUST ADD COFFEE.

Have you ever been stuck?

Have you ever needed change and needed it bad?

Have you ever wanted to go speeding down the highway with the radio blasting and the wind in your hair but found yourself mired in a rut with no tow truck in sight (and no charge left in your cell phone)?

Eighteen months ago I was mired in a rut just like that. I'd been an emotional zombie for about five months, reeling from an overdose of stress and loss. The stress came from a number of sources, the loss from the unexpected demise of an important — but wrong for me — relationship.

My friends could see I was sad. My family could see I was sad. Even my kids were worried about me.

One chilly fall evening I was browsing the

aisles at Barnes and Noble when I thumbed through a quirky-looking book titled *It's Called a Breakup Because It's Broken* by Greg Behrendt and Amiira Ruotola-Behrendt. The cover featured a tub of ice cream. The writing was humorous and conversational. Apparently this book had something going for it that I hadn't possessed in months, which was a personality. Figuring I could use a smile, I bought it.

The next day I went back and bought two different editions of another book coauthored by Greg Behrendt. That entire week, I read and reread these three little volumes. Everything else went untouched — the stack of books by my bedside, manuscripts, newspapers, mail, even the book *Eragon,* which Kacie, then eleven, had read, recommended, and let me borrow.

Soon I was into my second week of doing nothing but reading and rereading these three books. I practically had them memorized. I could hear Greg's and Amiira's voices in my sleep, reminding me that I wasn't the only person to have a relationship end painfully and that I could not only survive the experience, I could thrive and move on with style! By now, I didn't even have to read the pages in order anymore. I would simply grab one of the books, plop down on bed or chair, open the book to any page, and start reading.

One day as I was devouring the words before me, Kacie walked by. She stopped and observed me a moment, then said reflectively, "You know, normally, if I gave you one of my *favorite* books to read and it had been two weeks and you hadn't even looked at it, I might be sad. But I see what you're reading and I see how much it's helping you, so I don't mind at all."

She started to resume her trek into the kitchen when I stopped her. I said, "Wait a minute! You can tell? You can tell it's helping?"

"Yep, I can tell."

She left. I was ecstatic.

I *had* been feeling different. Stronger. Happier. Healthier. Like I was going to be okay after all. Now I knew it wasn't just my imagination. I *was* different. Even Kacie could tell.

It would be seven more months before I'd experience the final breakthrough in reclaiming my joy. (I describe that breakthrough in the last chapters of *Due to Rising Energy Costs, the Light at the End of the Tunnel Has Been Turned Off.*) But the change began in earnest that fall, with a book sporting a carton of cartoon ice cream on the cover.

Several weeks later I sat down at my computer to write Greg and Amiira a note expressing my heartfelt thanks. I must have gotten distracted by something (shocking, I know) because I never finished the note. Maybe one day I'll get around to it. Or, who knows, maybe one day they'll come across my thanks here, in these pages. Either way, I'm grateful for the book they wrote. Very grateful indeed.

In *The Rhythm of Life,* Matthew Kelly wrote about the transforming power of books. Here's what he had to say:

> Books change lives. I believe that with my whole heart. I like to ask people what was the greatest period of transformation in their life [and] . . . nine out of ten times, their eyes will light up and they'll say, "I was reading _____ and that book changed my life."[1]

It happens to the best of us. We find ourselves facing stubborn obstacles, longing for change and seemingly unable to get to where we want to be. Or maybe we can't quite put our finger on the problem, but we're discontented and restless, longing for . . . I don't know, something different. Something better.

When this happens, who ya gonna call? Forget Ghostbusters. Forget Spidey, Batman, or Wonder Woman. Trust me, you need a superhero of a different ilk. You need . . . *Change Agent*!

Books can be change agents. Other things

---

14. Watch an inspiring movie.

This one is easy. Rent an inspiring movie about someone who rose to the occasion and reinvented his or her life. Here are some of my favorites:

- *Baby Boom*
- *Rudy*
- *Bruce Almighty*
- *Cast Away*
- *Dead Poets Society*
- *Invincible*
- *The Final Season*

---

can be change agents too. The point is, change agents get things hopping. Whenever they are introduced into a situation, change agents create, you know, change. Sometimes change agents *initiate* change; sometimes they merely *accelerate* it. Either way, one thing is certain: when change agents show up on the scene, sooner or later *something's* going to happen.

CHANGE AGENTS REPORTING FOR DUTY

Put six teenagers who don't know one another in a room and you've got a half-dozen isolated kids texting friends on their phones. But throw in six cans of Silly String and — bingo! — you've got a party. Toss a couple of terrorizing tots into a suburban home and all you've got is, well . . . the neighbor kids from down the street. Introduce a Gestapo nanny and a television camera and — *voilà!* — you've got a hit reality show on your hands.

Let's face it, sometimes a well-timed catalyst can change everything. And the great thing is, you've got catalysts all around you.

I've already mentioned books, but let me say it again: Books are amazing catalysts. Books change people. They also can change entire societies. Just ask Harriet Beecher Stowe or Matthew, Mark, Luke, and John.

You want another example of a catalyst? How about love? I know a couple who were in their late twenties when they had their first baby. Janice recalls, "Rob and I had been big partiers when we met and hadn't changed much since then. But the moment our son was born, we took one look at our new baby and fell in love, and our stash went down the toilet. We hadn't been willing to do it for ourselves, but we could do it for him. We knew we were ready to grow up."

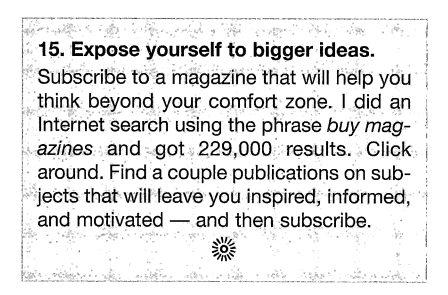

15. Expose yourself to bigger ideas.
Subscribe to a magazine that will help you think beyond your comfort zone. I did an Internet search using the phrase *buy magazines* and got 229,000 results. Click around. Find a couple publications on subjects that will leave you inspired, informed, and motivated — and then subscribe.

And speaking of love as a change agent, which one of us didn't go, "ahhhhhh," during that scene in *As Good as It Gets* when acerbic Jack Nicholson tells love interest Helen Hunt, "You make me want to be a better man"? Not to mention the last time you or I fell in love and went on crash diets and purchased new wardrobes as a result.

Where would we be without change agents? All you have to do is introduce love,

71

television cameras, new ideas, or even Silly String into pretty much any set of circumstances, and something's *definitely* gonna change.

YEEHAW! ROUND UP A HERD OF CATALYSTS

You know what most people do when they're stuck and longing for change? They start filling their free time with things that feel good or keep them occupied. You know, kind of like a pacifier. There's no mystery to the kinds of things I'm talking about, right? Whining. Watching TV. Comfort eating. Video games. Mindless Internet surfing. Shopping to dull our pain or restlessness or longing. All the stuff we do when we're simply trying to pass the time because we can't seem to get out of the rut we're in.

What would happen if you and I tried something new? What if we made a habit of filling our free time with *catalysts* instead of pacifiers? Even if we're not desperate for change at the moment, would we benefit from surrounding ourselves with positive change agents? You bet we would!

16. Leave your world and visit some-one else's for a while.

A change of context can jump-start change in your life. It stimulates a different way of thinking, inspires fresh ideas, opens your eyes to new options, and energizes you. Do yourself a favor and give serious consideration to something along these lines:

- Go on a missions trip.
- Volunteer your services in a different setting.
- Befriend someone who is very different from you.
- If you can't get away just now, read a biography of someone whose life is or was very different from your own.

Instead of settling for a pacifier, here's a sampling of things that can create or accelerate the changes we long for:

- Watching inspiring movies.
- Hanging out with wise mentors or good role models.
- Reading self-help or inspirational

books. (Every night before you fall asleep, spend a few minutes reading something designed to help you change or solve a problem in your life.)

- Putting motivational or self-help audio files on your iPod and listening while you drive, exercise, or do housework.
- Reading biographies or watching documentaries about people who have traits or accomplishments you'd love to emulate.
- Subscribing to magazines and journals created for professionals in your line of work.
- Attending conferences, retreats, and workshops.
- Finding people to love.
- Acquiring nonpeople to love. (Yes, pets are great catalysts. People who introduce loving furballs into their lives tend to have lower blood pressure, longer lives, and less depression!)
- Spending time with a professional counselor.
- Taking a college course.
- Spending more time with people who love and value you.
- Getting active in a church.
- Toning your body and attitude through exercise. (This is another great catalyst!

Introduce exercise into your life and you'll think more clearly, have more energy, feel happier, look sexier, and experience greater confidence in every area of life. Not a bad trade for an hour a day, huh?)

You, Only Different . . .

A change agent is anything that has the power to leave you different than you were before.

My daughter Kaitlyn has planned and organized a number of missions trips. In fact, tomorrow she and twenty-two other college students will travel to Utah on a trip she's been organizing for the past four months. She glows when she talks about the people in homes and shelters who will be receiving hope and help. She also glows when she talks about the growth and change such trips bring about in the lives of the students who go.

"I have yet to see anyone return from one of these trips the same person they were when we left. There's something about traveling to new places, learning to bond and work with your team, praying and seeing God answer those prayers, and reaching out in love to people in different cultures or circumstances. It changes you, enlarges your

75

understanding, your heart, your vision. After going on a missions trip, you couldn't see the world in the same old way even if you tried!"

You want change? Fill your life with experiences that make you act, think, or feel in ways that differ from your regular comfort zone. It takes a change of pace — a change agent — to leave you different than you were.

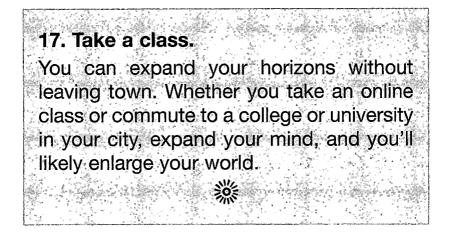

17. Take a class.
You can expand your horizons without leaving town. Whether you take an online class or commute to a college or university in your city, expand your mind, and you'll likely enlarge your world.

You can't always change your circumstances. At least not immediately. But change just one element — add a new person to the mix, ask a different question, try out a new assumption, react differently next time — and everything can shift. Circumstances are like a recipe: if just one ingredient is altered even a little, the balance is thrown off and the cookies turn out completely different!

I know a woman who is married to a man who is critical and demeaning. She says, "I can't change him." I told her, "Fine. Change you. Go to counseling. Read books. Join a support group. Learn how to speak the truth. Learn how to create safe, healthy boundaries for yourself. Learn how to be a stronger, healthier person. Learn how to love yourself. Stop protecting and accommodating his craziness. Get as emotionally healthy as you can. As you change, the current balance in your relationship will be thrown off. Something will shift and give. Who knows? He might even change as a result. But no matter what, as you work on you, it's going to change your *perspective* of your circumstances, the *impact* of your circumstances on your emotions, and very possibly even your actual *circumstances* themselves. But it starts with you."

The same advice goes for you and me. We can stagnate, or we can activate growth and change in our lives and in our circumstances. The likelihood of experiencing positive change jumps sharply as we surround ourselves with ideas and people and experiences that leave us different than we were before.

Tonight, nix the mindless Web surfing or

hypnotic eating in front of the television. Instead, fill your time with the kind of encouraging and motivating things that have the potential to rock your world.

The change'll do you good.

The Art of Change

Questions for personal reflection or group discussion:

When you are dissatisfied, do you fill your life with pacifiers — stuff that keeps you occupied or distracted without solving the problem at hand? If so, what are some of your favorite pacifiers?

Under what circumstances, if any, can a pacifier be a healthy option? How do you know when it's time to put down the pacifier and take action? How can you make that transition?

Name an experience or event that left you changed for the better. Maybe it was something you initiated, or perhaps it was completely unexpected. Is there a way you could create a similar experience, or at least similar results, in your life in the near future?

Do you feel overwhelmed when you think about replacing your pacifiers with catalysts? If so, why? What role could addictions or depression be playing in keeping you in a rut? If an addiction or depression is keeping you stuck, where can you go for help?

5

AUTOPILOT ROCKS. UNLESS, OF COURSE, YOU'RE POINTED IN THE WRONG DIRECTION.

WHAT YOU DON'T KNOW CAN HURT YOU

My dashboard clock flashed 6:44 as I drove south on Academy Boulevard. I had about fifteen minutes to get to my destination and — with Friday-night traffic jamming the roadways — I'd be lucky to make it in thirty.

Nevertheless, the evening promised to be a memorable one. Love was in the air. My gorgeous California cousin, Brenda, had flown into town that afternoon so my sister and I could set her up on a blind date with Mark, a handsome Colorado entrepreneur. The four of us were rendezvousing at 7:00 at a local country-western dance hall. Would our little matchmaking experiment end in fireworks? wedding bells? We would soon find out.

The whole thing had started a few weeks earlier when my sister Michelle came up with the wild idea of finding Brenda a husband. Not that our cousin can't get her own dates, but we thought it'd be fun to find her a Colorado husband so she would relocate and be our neighbor.

In order to make this dream come true, Michelle and I spent time on a dating Web site, selecting Mark from a bevy of eligible bachelors. After meeting him for lunch for a pre-date interview, we gave him the Siskel and Ebert two-thumbs-up and started making plans for Brenda to fly out.

But first we had to break the news to Brenda.

That night we called and told her what we'd done. After a substantial amount of screaming, scolding, and refusing to take part in our scheme, she relented and went to find her suitcase.

And now the big night was here.

The dashboard clock read 6:55. Between errands and meetings, I'd been on the road most of the day. I'd hoped for a few minutes to pull over and freshen up before joining our little party, but one glance at the time and I knew *that* wasn't going to happen.

In the seat next to me was the overnight bag I'd packed so I could spend the night at Michelle's. (What matchmaking scheme is complete without a follow-up slumber party for analysis and debriefing?) After reaching into the bag, I groped around until I found my toothbrush and toothpaste.

My plan was simple. Using the teensiest dab of toothpaste, I would brush my teeth, rinse my mouth with a swig of bottled water, then swallow. As far as I knew, ingesting a little toothpaste never killed anyone. It was a good plan. A very good plan. All I had to do was remember not to spit.

Never underestimate the power of habit.

HABITS: YOUR BRAIN AND BODY ON AUTOPILOT

I'll spare you the details of what happened next. I will, however, tell you that I ended up at the next stoplight with the heater cranked up and with me contorting my body so the front of my jeans was aligned with the hot-air vent. (You're no doubt wondering, *How in the world did you manage that?* My chiropractor asked me the same question the next day, and I couldn't explain it to him either.)

When I met up with Brenda and Michelle in the parking lot, Michelle tried to be encouraging. Looking at my saliva-soaked jeans, she said unconvincingly, "Why, it's hardly noticeable at all."

Brenda tried the silver-lining approach. "Look at it this way. No matter how close anyone gets, you'll be minty fresh."

Who knew that four decades of swishing

and spitting would create such an entrenched habit? And yet habits are awesomely powerful things. Once we get used to doing something a certain way, it can feel as though our brains and even our bodies are on autopilot. I'm sure you know what I'm talking about. You develop certain ways of acting, thinking, and speaking that come so naturally you don't have to think about them.

This can be a wonderful thing. After all, it would be pretty bothersome if every time you drove to work you had to think long and hard about whether to take that next turn or the one after. (Although, if you ever have occasion to brush your teeth on the way to work, paying close attention is probably a

18. Borrow some great habits.
You know that change you've been longing to make? Think of six people you know who are *already* doing it. Send each of them an e-mail and ask them to share with you three to five habits they practice that have enabled them to be so successful in that area. As you read their answers, ask yourself: what are they doing that I can incorporate into my life?

very good idea.)

My point is that the stuff we do on a regular basis becomes familiar, even rote. This is helpful in a lot of ways. For starters, habits enable us to multitask. The fact that our brains learn certain patterns and can repeat them almost automatically is the reason you and I can make dinner, talk on the phone, nag at our kids, and let the dog out — all at the same time and without skipping a beat.

Habits also free up time, resources, and attention so we can focus on more important things. If I could develop the simple habits of paying my bills on time, keeping my car keys in the same place, and keeping clutter at bay, my life would not only be a whole lot simpler, I'd also have a lot more time and energy to focus on stuff that really matters, like relationships. I can't tell you how many notes I've neglected to write to loved ones because I don't have three hours and twelve minutes to spare — twelve minutes to write the note and three hours to rummage around in the clutter of my home looking for envelopes, postage stamps, and my address book.

But habits have a darker side. They are the little anchors that keep us from straying from the lifestyle to which we've become accustomed, whether that lifestyle makes us happy or miserable. For example, the habit of overspending keeps us anchored to a lifestyle of financial stress. The habit of vegging out in front of the television and eating ice cream (instead of veggies) keeps us tethered to insecurities, plus sizes, and health risks. The habit of flinging harsh, belittling, or angry words at people we love keeps us in a pattern of strained, distant relationships. (Conversely, the habit of regular exercise keeps us healthy and active. The habit of always telling the truth keeps us enjoying the fruit of a life characterized by integrity.)

Whether we realize it or not, you and I have habits that have created, perpetuated, or are currently driving aspects of our lives that we love . . . as well as other aspects we'd love to change. If we practiced different habits, would our lives be any different? You bet. After all, someone who practices lying, stealing, and infidelity is going to live a very different life from someone who practices habits of integrity, faithfulness, generosity, and health.

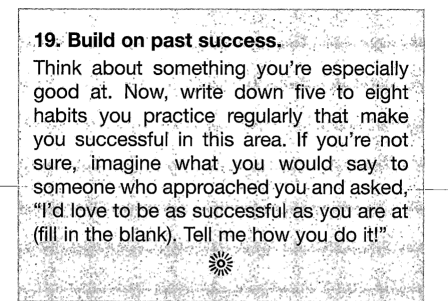

19. Build on past success.
Think about something you're especially good at. Now, write down five to eight habits you practice regularly that make you successful in this area. If you're not sure, imagine what you would say to someone who approached you and asked, "I'd love to be as successful as you are at (fill in the blank). Tell me how you do it!"

In talking about habits, Matthew Kelly writes, "Addictions are acquired by practicing a certain type of behavior often and excessively. Character is acquired by practicing certain types of behavior often and excessively."[1] In other words, our habits produce fruit. Are you hungry for change? Do you want your life to be sweeter than ever before? Then plant different habits.

I don't know what changes you want to make, so I can't tell you what old habits to discard and which new habits to embrace. But what you and I can do together is figure out how to identify habits we'd love to ditch and those we'd love to keep or develop, and then take a look at some really great strategies for making the switch.

Be Alert. The World Needs More Lerts.

Do you even *know* what habits you have?

Here's a simple example. I had no idea how many exclamation points I use when I'm writing e-mails until my exclamation point key broke on my laptop keyboard. Suddenly I became *very* aware of how often I reached for that key. In fact, the absence of exclamation points *so* impacts the tone of my e-mails that I felt it was necessary to add the following postscript to an e-mail I sent to my literary agent and my publicist:

> P.S. If something seems amiss in this e-mail, it's because my exclamation point key is broken and I'm being forced to end my sentences in a more reserved manner. I HATE it when that happens (insert exclamation point here).

Thank goodness Steve and Cat quickly e-mailed me back and included several dozen spare exclamation points that I could cut and paste into future e-mails as needed. I did this until yesterday, when I gave in and had a new keyboard installed.

My point is this: some habits are obvious.

We know what they are because we choose to do them. Like driving to the gym every day. Or stopping at the coffee shop every morning on our way to work. Or kissing our kids goodnight. Or having a bowl of ice cream every night before going to bed. Or doing laundry every Monday. Or feeling stressed about a book deadline in the very near future and eating cereal straight out of the box every time we're working at the computer and gaining four pounds in the process of writing the first three chapters alone. (I didn't just admit that, did I?) Some of these habits are healthy; some aren't. Either way, they come as no surprise. We know we're doing them.

Other habits aren't so obvious. In fact, we might not realize we've got them at all. But just as we track the direction of the unseen wind by watching the dance of the leaves, even if we don't see these habits, we can often figure out that they are there by observing their *impact.*

For example, name something you enjoy about your life. Maybe it's the fact that after so many years of marriage, you and your husband are still madly in love with each other. Now ask yourself, *What habits have contributed to my success?* Write down the first half dozen that come to mind. But don't stop now; keep thinking. Can you identify another five or six habits, things that one or both of you do that may be more subtle? Stuff you may not think about as contributing to your continuing love affair, but — now that you ponder it — has been contributing to your success all along?

Now look at your list. Interesting, isn't it? What you have spelled out in front of yourself are many of the habits that have made your marriage such an enjoyable success. Keep doing these things. When you experience a season when you feel disconnected, reread the list and see if you're still practicing these habits.

WHAT YOU DON'T KNOW *CAN* HURT YOU

We've identified a few habits that produce good fruit in our lives. Now let's pinpoint a few of the habits that are producing bitter fruit. These are the habits connected with the stuff in our lives we'd love to change.

For instance, my scale has been stuck in the same spot for several months, and I'd love to get past this frustrating plateau. Remember Bill Murray's predicament in the movie *Groundhog Day*? Well, they're making a sequel and they've asked me to play the starring role. It's called *Groundhog Diet,* and it's the story of a woman who's trying to lose weight except it doesn't matter how little she eats or how much she works out because apparently she's fallen into some weird cosmic time loop so that she's forced to live the same day over and over again, because every morning, when she stands on the scale, she ends up staring at exactly the same number from the previous morning.

This is something I'd love to change. So I made a list of the obvious habits that contribute to my little dilemma. The first is that I tend to eat healthy for about a week and then eat anything I want for three or four days. At this moment you're probably thinking, *Well, you're still eating healthy seven days out of ten. Why aren't you losing weight?* To which I can only reply, "Dear child, do not let the brevity of days in which I binge mislead you. Never underestimate the amount of food an experienced Binge Master can consume in a mere seventy-two-hour period."

Okay, so the three-day-binge thing isn't helping me. Neither is the fact that I'm not drinking enough water. Neither is the fact that some days I have to cut my walk short because I spent half the morning trying to remember what I did with my tennis shoes, music, sunglasses, sunscreen, and keys.

Now that I think about it, there are a number of more subtle habits that might be keeping me in Chubbyville:

- All the hidden calories I pour into my coffee every morning.
- The fact that I skimp on sleep. (If you want to know more about the surprising link between weight loss and sleep, read chapter 9 in my book *Chocolatherapy: Satisfying the Deepest Cravings of Your Inner Chick.*)
- My habit of bypassing the veggies and reaching instead for mass quantities of summer fruit. (Healthy, yes, but lots of sugar and calories.)
- Skipping breakfast and going as many hours as I can without eating. (Not eating might sound like a great weight-loss strategy, but all it does is make the ensuing binge virtually inevitable.)
- Not reading labels. (Many store-bought sugar-free foods are actually higher in carbs and calories than their sugarful cousins.)
- Putting stuff in my mouth to quiet stress or deal with loneliness or boredom.

Now that I've identified some of the habits I want to change, I can get to work.

What about you? Identify something in your life you'd love to change. Then make a list of some of the habits that contribute to the negative thing in your life — which you are now ready to change.

WHAT NEW HABITS COULD CHANGE YOUR LIFE FOR THE BETTER?

We've identified some of the habits we want to keep and other habits we want to change. But there's a third category of habits. These are habits we don't currently practice, but if we ever could add these babies to our repertoire of repetitive behavior, we'd certainly be thrilled with the results.

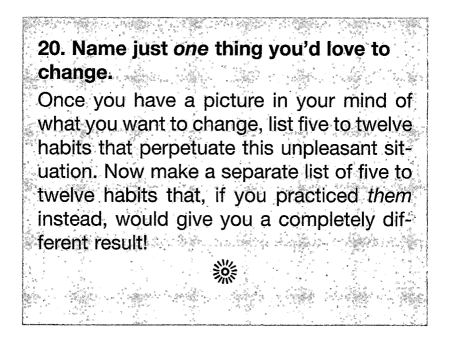

20. Name just *one* thing you'd love to change.

Once you have a picture in your mind of what you want to change, list five to twelve habits that perpetuate this unpleasant situation. Now make a separate list of five to twelve habits that, if you practiced *them* instead, would give you a completely different result!

I love people and their stories. I love observing their lives and trying to figure out why and how they do the things they do. So when I find people who have never struggled with something that's difficult for *me,* I'm anxious to learn their secret.

My sister's car is spotless. You could eat off the floor of her car (the fuzz from the floor mats might get in your mouth, but at least you'd know it was clean fuzz). So one day I asked her how she keeps her car so clean.

She held up a basket.

"This is my errand basket. If I'm out running around, I carry whatever I'm going to need for the day — shopping list, the CD I need to return, the bills I need to mail — in this basket instead of scattered all over the car. It keeps my car neat and tidy."

Immediately I pictured the several hundred random things that clutter the interior of my car. I said, "No kidding? That one little basket will solve my problem?"

Renee said, "Are you insane? Have you *seen* the inside of your car? If we took all the oddball things in your car and nuked them, the *ashes* wouldn't fit in this basket. I'm just telling you what works for *me. You're* going to have to rent a Dumpster."

Get ideas from other people who are suc-

21. Keep a journal.

Don't know what you're eating that's packing on the pounds? Can't figure out why you're always broke? Do you wonder where your time is going and why you can't seem to get around to doing the really important things you want to accomplish in your day?

Keeping a journal can help you identify hidden habits that are interfering with your life. You *can* embrace the changes you want to embrace — and getting a handle on what's really going on is a great way to begin!

✻

ceeding in an area of life where you want to improve. But keep in mind that you might need to take what you learn and tweak it a bit. If you stay alert, inquisitive, and teachable, you can acquire all sorts of cool new habits — habits that are reaping positive results in the lives of folks you know. And their good habits might just do the same for you.

In fact, if there's anything in *my* life you'd love to emulate, just ask me, and I'll be happy to describe the habits that made me the woman I am today.

One thing is certain, brushing my teeth while driving doesn't happen to be one of them.

The Art of Change

Questions for personal reflection or group discussion:

Discuss the statement, "Habits are the little anchors that keep us from straying very far from the lifestyle to which we've become accustomed, whether that lifestyle makes us happy or miserable." What experiences in your life support or contradict this thought?

Do you see any consistent patterns in your life? If you could redesign your life from scratch, which patterns would you reestablish and which would you drop like, well . . . like a bad habit?

Why are some habits harder to identify and break than others? Which are hardest to change, and which are easiest?

Why are habits crucial to achieving the changes you desire?

6

HOW CAN YOU STOP DOING THE THINGS THAT HOLD YOU BACK . . . AND START DOING THE THINGS THAT'LL GET YOU WHERE YOU WANT TO GO?

DOES THE NAME *PAVLOV* RING A BELL?

Whenever I'm working on my computer, I reach for the junk food.

Oh sure, I *try* to stem this mindless urge, but it's never easy. Every time I fire up my computer in an effort to capture a creative thought, my mouth opens wide and a rumbling murmur somewhere in my head says, *Feeeed meeee.* I'm starting to wonder if, at least for me, putting sentences together uses the same part of my brain as putting on mascara, because I can't seem to do either one with my mouth closed.

Since apparently I can only be creative while shoveling things into my mouth, I decided one day that I should at least try shoveling in healthy foods instead of empty calories. For several hours I tried munching on carrots, ice chips, sugar-free gum, and even tofu. But by afternoon, the Froot Loops in the pantry were not only still calling my name, they'd convinced the Twinkies, cheese puffs, and baking chocolate to join the chorus.

Recently I came up with a new strategy, and I think it might be working. I put a beautiful cut-glass candy bowl next to my computer and filled it with snacks. Not just *any* snacks, mind you. These were very special snacks — crunchy and flavored like chicken. The first time I did this, it took me less than an hour to absent-mindedly empty the dish. These days, the same bowl of snacks is lasting a couple days, sometimes longer. What this means is that my autopilot eating is slowing down. I'm starting to think about what I'm doing before stuffing things in my mouth.

Another week or two and my mindless nibbling should be completely under control. Which'll make a lot of people happy. Like my kids, who are tired of hearing me complain about my weight. And my therapist, who supports all — okay, some — of my zany self-improvement schemes. And definitely my dog, Buddy, who's been looking *really* confused every time I refill my candy bowl from his box of doggie treats.

In the last chapter, we talked about the importance of being aware of our habits and the results they produce in our lives. Habits bear fruit, with some producing fruit that is bitter and worm riddled, while other habits produce fruit that is sweet and satisfying.

But the million-dollar question remains: How can we make the switch? How can we stop doing the things that hold us back and start doing the things that will get us where we want to be? Once we've identified our habits — the ones we love, the ones we want to ditch, and the new ones we'd love to embrace — what do we do *then?*

Breaking old habits and embracing new ones isn't easy. But while it may not be easy, this stuff is learnable. In fact, with a little practice, we can actually get pretty good at choosing the habits that will produce the life we want. We can learn how to cast aside the habits that hurt our bodies, relationships, finances, and careers, and replace them with habits that leave us healthier, happier, and more secure than we've ever been.

Want better habits? Here are five things to keep in mind.

1. Know your brain.

The first thing to keep in mind is this: habits

are not just about willpower; habits are also about re-creating patterns in your brain. So get to know how your brain works. (Notice I said *how,* not *if.* Although if you're anything like me, there are days you'll want to run a check on that too.)

Every time we take an action, think a thought, feel an emotion, or relive a memory, neurons in our brains are fired in a particular pattern. Every time we repeat that action, thought, or feeling, that pattern becomes more entrenched in our brains. Pretty soon all we have to do is start down the path of that familiar feeling, thought, or action — like my little behind-the-wheel tooth-brushing fiasco discussed in chapter 5 — and our brains go on autopilot and attempt to complete the thought or action the same way we've done it tens of thousands of times before. This is called a habit.

This is a good system. It's how we learn. It's why things feel more natural the more we do them. It's the reason a concert pianist can perform a tremendously difficult piece without striking a false note. It's the reason Tiger Woods can consistently make winning shots. It's also the reason you and I can put on mascara while driving to work without having to watch ourselves in the rearview mirror.

Unfortunately, the same brain functions that make us efficient when it comes to wielding golf clubs and mascara wands can make us efficient at bad habits as well. This is why we can feel "triggered" to respond the same way we've responded a hundred times before, even if we meant to respond *differently* this time around!

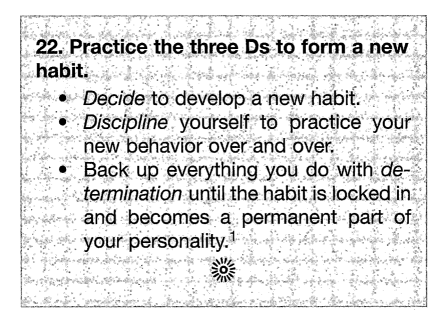

22. Practice the three Ds to form a new habit.
- *Decide* to develop a new habit.
- *Discipline* yourself to practice your new behavior over and over.
- Back up everything you do with *determination* until the habit is locked in and becomes a permanent part of your personality.[1]

For example, remember when your boss stopped by your office and asked if you had finished the spreadsheet for the board meeting next week? She used the same disapproving tone of voice your mom used with you when you were a kid. No wonder you had a sudden urge to yell, "The spreadsheet isn't due until tomorrow, so get off my back,

Mom!" (Your boss, of course, is not named Mom.) That's a conditioned response, a habit trained by years of practice. And in this instance, it wouldn't earn you a promotion.

What other response patterns do we have? When someone criticizes us, do we lash out without thinking? When we walk into a movie theater, do we automatically crave popcorn?

The bad news is that training ourselves to stop going down the path of our old habits — and blazing new habit patterns to replace them — isn't easy. At least not at first. In the beginning, it takes commitment and concentration because we're taking the path of most resistance. We're going against the grain of established grooves in our brains.

The good news is that the more we practice new habits, the more natural they feel. And in time — and with enough practice — our new, healthy habits can feel as familiar and automatic as our old, lousy habits!

Don't get discouraged, thinking it will be this much work forever. The trick is to find ways to keep doing the better habit (and keep *not* doing the bitter habit) until you wear a new groove in your brain. Once that happens, you'll be moving to the groove, baby. You'll be moving to the groove.

2. Keep taking the new path.

When you're trying to create a new habit, half the battle is simply remembering to go down the newly blazed path of your new habit before your brain sends you down the well-trodden path of your old habit. Tie a string around your finger, enter a reminder in your PDA, set your phone alarm, or slap sticky notes all over your bathroom mirror. Pretty soon your brain will take over, and you won't need all these reminders. But until then, think of external reminders as part of your brain because they'll be doing a job that your brain will, eventually, take over and start doing automatically.

Here are a couple of examples of what this looks like.

After my sister reorganized her kitchen pantry, she wanted to help her family learn where everything went. She put labels on the front of her kitchen cabinets so there would be no question which cabinet contained frying pans, cookie sheets, Tupperware, and more.

My dad uses sticky-note reminders, but I'm not organized enough to keep sticky notes handy. For half the school year I drove around with the words, "Pick Kacie up from school today," scrawled on my rearview mirror in eyebrow pencil.

23. Go overboard.

When learning a new habit, don't be afraid to exaggerate your new behavior. Then, if you're stressed or nervous and find yourself performing your new habit with less gusto, you'll still be in the ballpark. For example, when my daughter was learning her lines for a Christmas play, she was having a hard time remembering to speak up until I sat in the next room and made her yell her lines so I could hear them. After a week of *that,* it was easy for her to project in a more normal fashion from the stage.

❈

A woman told me she was tired of snapping at her family when she was feeling grumpy. To change this habit, she dubbed one of her rattiest old robes the Grumpy Robe. Whenever she wore it, her family knew Mom needed some space! The robe also reminded this woman that, at the moment, she was like a rubber band — stretched and ready to deliver a painful snap — and that she didn't *have* to react on autopilot. She could make a different choice, and wearing this fuzzy, tangible reminder helped keep that thought at the forefront of her mind.

Use whatever you need to use, as long as it reminds you to practice the new habit you want to develop, whether that habit is remembering to take the trash out on Monday mornings or remembering not to throw a tantrum in front of your kids. And just think! Before long your brain will be regrooved and you won't have to wear a ratty robe just to remind yourself to act civil.

Won't it be nice to wear normal clothes to the supermarket again?

3. Get a buddy.

With my twenty-one-year-old daughter back at college, I needed a new walking buddy. I enlisted my mom, and it has been great. On mornings she's tempted to sleep in, I call her. On mornings I'm in the mood to blow it off, she calls me. This has gotten us both on the trail on a lot of mornings when one or both of us might have stayed home in bed!

There's one danger I can see with the buddy system. If you really want to, you can use it as an excuse to slough off. You can end up saying things like, "Well, I *would* have done this-or-that except my buddy didn't call me." It's great to use your buddy as inspiration and motivation, but don't put the responsibility for your change on her shoulders. It's still up to you. Take ownership of the change you want to make . . . then do it.

4. Concentrate your efforts.

The more practice you get in a short time frame, the more of an impression it'll make on your brain. Sorry for the comparison, but it's kind of like training a dog. I've been trying to train Buddy, our Boston terrier, to stay in a certain part of the house (because he tends to leave souvenirs in other parts of the house). Sure, I could do my "no, no, bad dog" routine every few days when I remember to monitor his whereabouts and catch him in restricted territory, but what if his memory is as bad as mine? Will he really get the message, or will he miss the point and wonder why I randomly restrict him to the part of the house that doesn't double as a doggie toilet?

Luckily for all of us, my daughter and nephews came to the rescue. They spent half an afternoon working with Buddy, teaching him not to cross the imaginary line separating the two zones. They weren't allowed to call or beckon him over the threshold, but they certainly did everything else, including dancing, eating bacon, and barking like dogs. And every time Buddy tried to enter the No Dog Zone, he got to hear my "no, no, bad dog" routine. Every time he remembered the rules, he got a treat.

Two hours and thousands of "no, no, bad dog's" and puppy treats later, Buddy was a new canine. You might even say he had a new leash on life.

In the course of just one afternoon, the new groove in his brain got reinforced and his behavior began to change. In other words, Buddy formed a new habit after a single afternoon of concentrated regrooving — the same habit that had eluded him during months of hit-and-miss scolding.

Kacie, Connor, Hunter, and Isaac created opportunities for Buddy to practice and deepen the desirable groove in his brain. What if you and I did the same? What if we created opportunities to practice whatever new habit we want to reinforce?

24. Disrupt a well-worn rut.

It doesn't take much for your brain to fall back into the rut of a well-established habit. Look for "cues" in your environment that direct your brain onto the path of a bad habit. When you identify a cue, change your environment. Either remove the cue or make it hard for your brain to follow through. Need to break a chat room habit? Move your computer to a more public location in your home. Junk food habit? Empty your pantry of tempting foods. TV habit? Turn your television so it faces the wall. Smoking habit? Give your cigarettes to your neighbor so you have to walk across the street to get a smoke. Disrupting an old pattern can make it harder for your brain to go on autopilot.

***

I heard about a man who wanted to show food who was boss. Whenever he sat down to a meal, he chatted with his family and left his food untouched for five minutes, just to practice his willpower. He could have skipped the practice and waited until he was faced with some gooey, fattening dessert to start practicing his willpower . . . But he didn't. He found a way to practice self-control three or four times every day on harmless stuff like, oh, I don't know, green beans and meatloaf. You can bet by the time he was faced with some fabulous Death by Chocolate confectionary, he was ready!

And if you *can't* practice more often in real life, practice in your head. Three or four times a day, close your eyes and picture yourself having mastered the habit you want to ingrain in your brain. Imagine yourself turning down that dessert or saying no to the very nice woman who phones every year and talks you into ironing six hundred cloth napkins for her organization's Christmas fundraiser. Imagine yourself treating your husband the way you did when you were newlyweds, or speaking in public without white-knuckling the podium, or passing the makeup counter at your favorite department store without blowing three hundred bucks.

Imagine yourself standing tall, brimming with inner peace and confidence. Imagine yourself humming while you wash dishes, contented instead of resentful at the mundane tasks in your busy day. Imagine saying the words, "I forgive you" — and really meaning it.

5. Use stomach-turning associations.

You want to end a troublesome habit? Start associating it with something gross. Make it as disgusting as you can. My aunt Jeanette joined SmokEnders in the 1980s to help her give up cigarettes. She recalls that in the first weeks of the program, she was allowed to smoke but had to use a coffee can filled with water as her ashtray. And she was instructed *not* to change the water.

"You have no idea how disgusting a can of water filled with floating butts and ashes can become!" she told me. "The more I had to look at that can of filthy water and associated it with smoking, the less attractive my old habit started to become."

You want disgusting? A candy dish filled with dog biscuits is pretty disgusting. I can't tell you how many times I sat down at my computer and went into autopilot, immediately craving something to nibble. Time and time again I mindlessly reached my hand toward the candy dish until it dawned on me that I was about to eat dog food. Yuck! Instant revulsion! Trust me when I tell you that it was a great way to bring my autopilot program to a screeching halt. As soon as I started associating the urge to nibble with canine kibble, bingo! Problem solved. The same principle works in reverse. Is there a habit you'd love to embrace? Start associating it with stuff you enjoy. For example, I hate housework but love music and pretty things. When I combine all three, practicing good housework habits suddenly doesn't seem so distasteful. Although it has led to some interesting moments . . .

About a month ago Kacie attended a dinner theater with a friend and her family. The evening ran long, and it was nearly midnight before she got dropped off at home. I happened to be washing dishes when she walked in. Immediately she started to laugh.

"What's so funny?" I demanded.

"Lexi's aunt felt really bad when the evening went longer than planned. She asked if we'd wake you up, what with me coming home so late and all. I said, 'No way.' I told her you never go to bed at normal times. I told her sometimes I wake up in the middle of the night and I can hear you moving furniture, hanging pictures, or sawing things. And sure enough, here it's midnight and I open the front door and every light's on in the house, there's music blaring, and you're washing dishes while wearing your hip scarf and belly dancing. Why am I not surprised?"

---

25. Get your ducks in a row.
When learning a new habit, make it as easy as possible! One way is to get everything ready — all the ingredients (clothing, tools, equipment) you'll need — the night before. That way, when it's time to practice your new habit tomorrow morning, you won't get distracted.

Are you trying to get in the habit of going to the gym every morning? Collect everything you need — gym shoes and clothes, shampoo, towel, car keys, water bottle, iPod — the night before so that when morning arrives you're ready to go! Do you want to develop the habit of paying each bill the same day it arrives in your mailbox? Stock your desk with supplies ahead of time so you know exactly where to find everything you need — bills, stamps, envelopes — when you need them.

I have two thoughts related to this little incident. My first thought is, *How cool is this?* All you have to do is start associating a dreaded duty with a little rhythm and beauty and you've got it made. Washing dishes is far from my favorite pastime. But pairing it with a little Electric Oasis and a jingly lavender hip scarf forms a new groove in my brain. Suddenly housework is no longer the hated chore from the black pit. It takes on a whole new element of fun.

My second thought is that my kids are going to need *so* much therapy.

FEEL LIKE YOU'RE IN A RUT? YOU HAVE NO IDEA!

You and I have great plans, don't we? We want to eat healthier, lose weight, slow our spending, start exercising, worry less, love more, stop hurting, and pull off a dozen other wonderful transformations. There's a good chance that any great change we want to make will require the development of a new set of habits that support that change. And you know what *that* means, don't you?

It means that — at first — making the transition will feel unnatural. It might be difficult. That's what it feels like any time we are in the process of ending one habit and starting another.

The good news is that the "unnatural" feeling associated with a new habit is temporary. That's the whole nature of habits. They may start out difficult, but with enough practice there's a good chance they'll end up feeling like a second skin.

Come to think of it, that explains a lot. Lately I've had the strangest craving for a Milk-Bone.

The Art of Change

Questions for personal reflection or group discussion:

Do you believe bad habits are easier to form than good ones? Why or why not? Don't the same principles apply to both?

Do habits start in your actions or in your thoughts? Give an example.

What role can making yourself accountable play in breaking old habits or creating new ones? What does the word *accountability* mean to you?

If someone you know was trying to break an old habit or establish a new one, what is the best advice you could give her?

Discuss the biblical passage in which Paul confesses that the things he doesn't want to do, he can't help doing. And the things he wants to do, he has trouble accomplishing (Romans 7:15–23). Is there anything in his experience you can apply and use in your own life?

What relationship, if any, is there between habits and sin? What solution does Paul propose?

7

PROCRASTINATORS OF THE WORLD, UNITE! TOMORROW.

WARNING: DATES IN CALENDAR ARE CLOSER THAN THEY APPEAR

I am the Queen of Procrastination. No, really. The only reason I'm not wearing a crown at the moment is because I haven't gotten around to ordering one.

Less than two weeks before a *huge* writing deadline, I should have been working. Instead I spent the day looking up pirate-related Web sites (check out www.pirate parenting.com) and e-mailing them to a half-dozen friends. Granted, these friends are all writers — in fact, they meet at my house every six weeks or so to talk about the blessings and banes of our chosen profession. So if anyone can appreciate how far a person will go to avoid writing, it's going to be these folks.

At some point I decided the pirate links were too good not to share with as many people as possible and began copying my sisters on everything. In the middle of all this e-mailing, my phone rang. I picked up the phone and growled, *"Arrrrrrrr."*

My sister Renee said, "Working hard on your book?" I called her a landlubber and asked if she wanted to meet me for grog at a local coffee shop.

She sighed. "I'm always amazed that your house hasn't been repossessed yet."

So you can see the problem.

I also struggle with paying my bills. Even when I have money sitting in my bank account, I hate paying bills. As due dates approach, I shake a stern finger at myself (best done in front of a mirror unless I want to risk spraining my wrist) and say sharply, "Tonight you're sitting down at the kitchen table and writing out those bills!"

I do this every day for several weeks until the phone calls start. I'm not sure it's a good sign when you're on a first-name basis with the collection departments of all your utility companies, but I kind of like the phone calls. I'm always very cooperative with the collection agents on the other end. In fact, I'm downright grateful.

"Thank you for calling," I always say. "You have no idea how helpful this is! I hate writing out checks, but I'm very happy to pay this bill over the phone and am so glad you were so thoughtful to have called!"

---

26. Go to Amazon.com and order *Eat That Frog!* by Brian Tracy.

Get "addicted" to the great feeling of accomplishment! Brian Tracy will tell you exactly how to tackle and complete distasteful tasks first thing in the morning. We really can train ourselves to act quickly — and independently — of the negative feelings that keep us in bondage to unfinished business in our lives.

✳

Once I asked the telephone company if they could put my name on a list and call me automatically every month before my bill was overdue. They told me to grow up and mail my check in on time. But that's okay. Sometimes even in the best relationships you have to simply agree to disagree.

I was happy with this system until I decided to buy a house. That's when Brad, my mortgage broker, said, "Karen, your income is fine and you always pay your bills, but all these late pays are killing your credit score. In fact, I don't know if I can find a lender willing to consider a score as low as yours."

Since my former husband had always handled our finances, all this credit score stuff was news to me. I frowned. "Really? So what kind of credit scores do lenders look for?"

"Something with more than two digits would be a start."

The good news is that I got the house I wanted. The bad news is that every month I have to drive to the warehouse district at midnight, find a man carrying a violin case, and hand him a trash bag stuffed with un-marked bills. But I get to refinance in a few months, and you'll be happy to know I've been trying *really* hard to pay all my bills on time. In fact, I haven't needed any re-minder calls in almost two years. Sure, I miss talking with the friends I made in the collection industry, but it feels really good to have a decent credit score again. And all it took was making an ironclad decision to pay my bills on time — and then *actually doing it.*

Apparently even pirates have to play by the rules now and then.

ONE REASON WE PROCRASTINATE: IMPERFOBIA

It has taken me years to figure out this procrastination thing. I've finally come to the realization that one of the reasons I procrastinate is because I'm a closet perfectionist. This does not mean I have perfect closets, unless you think perfect closets should be largely vacant because they contracted some sort of virus that makes them, on a daily basis, spew their contents all over the bedroom floor. (This describes the relationship between my closet and the rest of my bedroom. In fact, close friends who have seen my bedroom are convinced that such a closet virus actually exists. One friend also commented, "So this is what it would look like if a bomb went off in a thrift shop.")

When I say I'm a closet perfectionist, I mean I'm a perfectionist, but you might not realize it at first glance. Even *I* didn't realize it for the longest time. I thought I was the complete opposite of a perfectionist. I was convinced that I was something more along the lines of an "incompletist." I say this because I have yet to completely finish anything I've ever started.

When you visit my house you'll notice that the draperies in the living room are hung but not hemmed.

Only half the trim in the hallway is painted.

> ### 27. Take advantage of a truly phenomenal to-do list.
>
> Go to www.karenlinamen.com, and download the most amazing to-do list in the world! I designed this list based on recommendations in Brian Tracy's book *Eat That Frog!* It's free. It works. You'll love it. What more can I say?
>
> ☼

My closet doors are beautifully hand-rubbed with a dozen shades of camels, butters, and browns, but I've never gotten around to reattaching the doorknobs.

I buy and hang the cutest picture frames. And I have high hopes of, one day, filling them with family photos. In the meantime, it's just one more project partially done, although I have to admit that the models in the fake photos make handsome additions to our family.

So why — when I'm surrounded by such *imperfection* — have I come to the conclusion that I'm a perfectionist? I am a perfectionist because I suffer from a condition known as imperfobia. In other words, I'm terrified of imperfection. And because I buy into the unrealistic idea that every finished project has to be a *perfect* project . . . Well, you can see the problem.

This is why I find it more comfortable to live with unfinished projects, because who in her right mind could expect perfection from something that's not done yet?

And yet . . .

This habit of never finishing anything I start keeps me from being able to follow through on my decisions. It also keeps my brain busy juggling dozens of loose ends.

I don't know if you're a closet perfectionist, but I can safely assume that you procrastinate on occasion — since everybody does. My question to you is, Why do *you* procrastinate? What keeps you from following through with the things you know you need to do — and in many cases *want* to do — so you can finally embrace the changes you've been dying to make?

PROCRASTINATION: AVOIDING AN ACTION OR AN EMOTION?

I've struggled with procrastination for years. I've read books and articles on the subject. I've researched it on the Internet. But when I read the following words by Dr. Kevin P. Austin, psychologist and director of Student Counseling Services at the California Institute of Technology, I knew I was onto something. Austin wrote, "People procrastinate because they experience emotions they don't want to feel when they attempt to do things."[1]

As soon as I read these words, something in my brain went, *"Yes!"* It's true. I don't procrastinate to avoid *doing* things — even unpleasant things. Instead, I procrastinate to avoid *feeling* unpleasant emotions, like my imperfobia-driven panic that whatever I'm about to attempt might not turn out all that great.

What are some of the unpleasant emotions that crop up? You and I may feel . . .

- afraid
- helpless
- powerless
- overwhelmed
- controlled
- sad
- rebellious
- embarrassed
- discouraged
- anxious
- guilty
- disinterested
- resentful
- bored
- insecure

123

- exhausted
- ashamed
- inferior

What does this look like? I checked with various people I know, and here are some examples I gleaned from their lives (and from mine).

A friend put off seeing a doctor about her acne because just thinking about making an appointment reminded her how unattractive she felt. Procrastinating kept that feeling at bay.

Another friend put off dieting because the thought of sticking with a diet plan made her feel controlled and restricted, feelings she could avoid by procrastinating.

28. Don't ask, "Why?" Ask, "What?"

Are you procrastinating on something? Don't ask yourself, *Why am I putting this off?* That question appeals to your intellect, and your intellect isn't the problem. Your intellect *knows* you need to be doing this project and that there's really no good reason to be putting it off. In fact, intellectually, you may even realize that by putting it off you are merely making the problem bigger and uglier than it was yesterday. So your intellect isn't holding you back.

Instead ask yourself, *What emotion do I feel when I think about tackling this project?* Now you're getting somewhere. When you can answer this question honestly, you're onto something that may help you address the root of your procrastination and get past it.

❋

A colleague has been putting off an important phone call he needs to make that will help unravel the financial knot he's tied up in. With his procrastination, is he consciously trying to avoid the benefits of greater freedom in his life? Not at all. He longs for resolution. His procrastination is orchestrated to help him avoid the unpleasant emotions — embarrassment and failure — he feels when he merely *thinks* about the problem at hand.

I once put off paying a parking ticket until the very last minute because every time I thought about finding the envelope and stamps necessary to mail in my payment, I felt overwhelmed by the lack of organization in my home. By procrastinating, I avoided feeling discouraged and defeated by my cluttered work space.

My neighbor puts off calling a service to mow her lawn. It's not because she can't afford it or because she *likes* a lawn that resembles an enormous, green, shaggy mammal. No, she puts off making that phone call because every time it crosses her mind, she feels resentful that her husband spends Saturday mornings golfing instead of helping her around the house.

Finally, my dad has been after me for three weeks to make arrangements to pick up the extra set of tires and rims I'm buying from Scott, the owner of Genesis Salon where I get my hair done. When I kept procrastinating, Dad figured I was broke and offered to pay for the tires. When I procrastinated some more, he figured I didn't have a way to haul the tires home and offered to pick them up in his truck. The truth is, I wanted the tires and I had the money and the transportation needed to make it happen. Instead, my procrastination was all about avoiding the *feeling* I got whenever I thought about calling Scott. You see, three weeks ago I missed my hair appointment. So the emotion I experience when I think about calling Scott is, well, some combination of chagrin and dismay. Not that Scott would make me feel bad for missing an appointment — he's a gracious soul and a friend to boot. But still . . . Well, you get the picture.

Insecure about our looks. Controlled and restricted. Embarrassed and inadequate. Overwhelmed. Resentful. Chagrined and dismayed. When any of these feelings appear on the horizon, is it any wonder we sail the other direction?

CAP'N KAREN'S TIPS FOR TAKING ROGUE EMOTIONS CAPTIVE

More often than not, the advice given to chronic procrastinators is to manage our time better. How useless is that? If we knew how to manage our time, we'd already be doing it! Plus, as we just discussed, time management is *not* the core issue.

Actually, I'm all for better time management. And frequently I'm pretty good at it. I say this because I almost always manage to find time to do the things that make me feel good. And if good time management frees up more time in my day, great! That means I'll have even *more* time to do the things that make me feel good!

We don't procrastinate because we're short on time. We procrastinate because we're short on better ways to manage the unpleasant emotions we've attached to certain tasks.

29. Try the sitcom solution.

Devote half an hour every day to completing a project or making a dream come true. That's right, just thirty minutes a day. That's the time it takes to watch a rerun of *Gilligan's Island.* You'll be surprised at what you can accomplish by applying a few minutes a day over an extended period of time!

How can we stop procrastinating and start doing the things we need to do to bring about the changes we crave? I came up with five ways you and I can begin to manage the emotions that fuel our procrastination. Because one of my recent procrastination episodes involved pirates, I figured we needed a good piratey word to use as an acronym to help us remember the five principles. And can anyone think of a better piratey word than *Arrrr?*

So here it is: Cap'n Karen's guide to managing the rogue emotions that encourage procrastination (and one of the few times you can get good advice while spelling the word *Arrrr*):

1. Acknowledge the emotion.

Recently I came across one of my to-do lists from eleven months ago. Eleven months. That's almost an entire year. The ancient list looked uncannily familiar. And for good reason. No less than nine of the eleven items on the list *are still on my current to-do list.* That's right. My to-do list for this week is, for the most part, exactly the same as my list from a year ago.

You don't believe me? Call Dave Barry. He'll tell you I'm not making this up.

This begs the question, why? But I've learned the hard way that there's no use asking myself — or any other procrastinator — the obvious question: Why are you putting this off? This is because we don't have a good answer. The best we can come up with are excuses. (Try telling someone you haven't gotten around to completing a half-hour task *over the course of an entire year* because you can't find the time. It doesn't fly.) I'm convinced chronic procrastinators aren't *trying* to be difficult or evasive. We would give you a straight answer if we could. Unfortunately we can't answer the why question because we don't *know* why.

So we need to ask the question a different way: "What emotions do you feel when you think about tackling this project?" Sometimes, if we're willing to be honest, that's a question we can answer! The next time you find yourself procrastinating, don't ask *why.* Instead, ask *what.* "What emotion do I feel whenever I think about tackling this project?"

You might find that your answer goes something like this . . .

- "I feel confused by the process, and I'm unclear about the best next step to take in order to get this done."
- "I feel panicked that I might not succeed."
- "I feel dread over what I have to go through to get this completed."
- "I feel fear at what I might discover."
- "I feel bad about myself because . . ."
- "I feel embarrassed or ashamed over . . ."
- "I feel vulnerable because . . ."

The emotion that keeps you from tackling one project might be different from the emotion that keeps you from completing something else. So ask yourself the *what* question for each thing you're putting off. As you identify each emotion that keeps you in bondage to a life overrun with loose ends, you may find yourself better prepared to decide whether to *relieve* that emotion, *replace* it, or *reject* it.

Let's take a look at all three.

2. Relieve the emotion.

When you think about creating that long-overdue Web site for your business, do you feel overwhelmed because you don't have a clue how to begin? Then get a clue. The way I figure it, you've got two choices: you can spend six months avoiding the overwhelmed feeling, *or* you can get rid of the over-whelmed feeling within a few days or even hours by making a few phone calls, signing up for a class, or browsing Web sites for the information you need to get this project underway, delegated, or completed.

When you think about calling the guy who does your hair, do you feel embarrassed because you missed your appointment a month ago? Here are your choices: you can spend the next six months avoiding that embarrassed feeling (while your roots grow out and make you look fifteen years older than you really are), *or* you can relieve that feeling in thirty seconds by making a phone call and starting your conversation with the words, "Hi, Scott. I'm *so* sorry I missed my appointment last month. I need to reschedule and, while we're on the phone, figure out a

time to pick up the tires you've got for sale."
Ta-da. Problem solved.

Here are some actions you can take to relieve other negative emotions:

Feeling overwhelmed by a particular project?

- Divide the project into baby steps that feel doable.
- Get a timer and work on the project twenty minutes a day.
- Find a buddy to help you do this thing.

Feeling overwhelmed by life?

- Ask yourself if you are overbooked.
- Make a phone call and cancel something.
- Check your work habits: is your desk so messy that you can't find the stamps you need to mail the check to pay for your parking ticket?

Feeling bored and looking for more interesting distractions?

- Train yourself to tackle and finish things quickly. Sure, it might be a boring task, but it's going to get even more boring if you stretch it out over weeks or months.

Whenever you think of tackling a project you've been putting off, do you feel exhausted?

- Get more sleep.
- Chronic exhaustion can be a sign of depression. Go online to www.depression-screening.org, and complete the questionnaire about clinical depression. If your score indicates that you might be struggling with depression, make an appointment to see a professional.
- Be honest with yourself. Exhaustion can also be a sign that this is something you really don't want to do. Admittedly, sometimes we don't have a choice about certain things (like paying speeding tickets). But sometimes we volunteer for or commit to optional things that we don't have the time or desire to finish. When we are honest with ourselves (and with others) about what we really have the time and desire to tackle, it can help us eliminate the negative feelings we experience when we've been roped into unwanted (and nonessential) commitments.

Bottom line: once you've identified the

emotion holding you back, is there an action you can take that will resolve, relieve, or eradicate that feeling?

If there is, do it.

3. Reject the emotion.

If you can't relieve the negative emotion that is keeping you from doing something you really need or want to do, you may want to try this: simply reject the emotion.

I say *simply,* but I know it can be anything but simple.

As a general rule, I don't advocate denying our emotions. But when that emotion is keeping you from completing a goal or task you want to complete, ignoring or denying it can be a good idea — at least until your goal is met. Then go ahead and revisit that emotion and see if it needs to be explored.

How do I reject the negative emotions that keep my feet to the fires of procrastination?

Self-talk is one approach. I speak to myself, out loud, often while driving or walking, and give myself whatever straight talk or pep talk I need to counteract, neutralize, or even banish that negative emotion.

For instance — oh, let's see, what have I been procrastinating on lately — wait, I know. Getting my taxes done. It's already June, and I have yet to file. I filed for an extension, but still . . . I need to get it done. Problem is, every time I think about it I feel overwhelmed, not to mention the shame and dread. So when I was on my five-mile walk the other day, this is what I told myself: "Karen, everybody feels overwhelmed by the paperwork. Everybody feels bad, like they *should* have filed sooner or *should* have kept better mileage records. And everyone dreads the whole kit and caboodle. So your feelings, in this case, don't mean much. They don't mean you can't do this. They don't mean you're a bad person. They just mean you're normal. So set those puppies to one side and get going. You're bigger than this little unpleasant task that everyone in America manages to do and conquer. So go. Do. Conquer."

30. Disengage your brain.

Do you keep putting off something important you need to do? Your problem could be that you're thinking too much. If your brain is filled with thoughts about how huge this project is or how far you still have to go or even how sad/bad/fearful/anxious you feel when you think about getting started, no wonder you keep putting it off! At this rate, Indiana Jones would put it off!

The solution? Stop thinking about it. Disengage your brain. For instance, don't think about how much you dread the stairstep machine. Just put your brain in neutral as you grab your gym bag and head out the door.

With practice, you can become skilled at taking action and following through on your decisions without sabotaging your progress with negative thoughts and emotions.

❈

If that doesn't work, I try outrunning my feelings. I try doing several things at once very quickly, throwing my unpleasant task into the mix and hoping I don't notice that I'm doing it. In other words, I'm distracting myself, forcing myself to think about doing other things at the same time, so my mind doesn't linger on whatever negative emotions I've attached to the task at hand.

It might take days or decades, but don't give up. Keep working at discrediting and discarding the emotions that fuel your procrastination so you can get on with the business of making your dreams come true.

4. Replace the emotion.

It makes sense that we would think about a project before jumping in. We might need to gather supplies or check the calendar or line up a friend to help us. There is a certain amount of advance thinking that takes place before we get started.

But why do we tend to think and feel *negative* things? If we're going to bother thinking things through ahead of time, why not think and feel something *positive* that propels us to finish the project with panache?

One way to do this is to get *addicted to accomplishment.*

---

31. Hire an antiprocrastination assistant.

Sometimes when I'm *really* procrastinating and just can't force myself to do what I need to do, I arrange for someone to simply be there. She doesn't have to do a thing — just sit with me while I tackle the thing I've been avoiding. The presence of another person who knows what it is I'm supposed to be doing helps keep me on task.

137

At times I arrange a freebie by asking one of my sisters or a friend to show up and keep me on track. Other times I hire a temporary assistant to come work with me in my office — her presence inspires me to stay busy doing the things I need to be doing. Once I asked my mom to just sit with me at the kitchen table while I paid bills.

I return the favor too. For example, when my sister kept putting off scheduling a critical mammogram, I told her I was coming over and sitting in her living room until she made the call.

Sometimes we all need a little handholding. Don't be afraid to enlist some moral support when you just can't seem to get it done on your own!

According to success coach Brian Tracy, every time we finish a task we feel a "surge of energy, enthusiasm and self-esteem. The more important the completed task, the happier, more confident and more powerful you feel about yourself and your world."

Tracy adds:

The completion of an important task triggers the release of endorphins in your brain. These endorphins give you a natural "high." The endorphin rush that follows successful completion of any task makes you feel more positive, personable, creative and confident.

You can actually develop a "positive addiction" to endorphins and to the feeling of enhanced clarity, confidence and competence that they trigger. When you develop this addiction you will, at an unconscious level, begin to organize your life in such a way that you are continually starting and completing ever more important tasks and projects. You will actually become addicted, in a very positive sense, to success.[2]

5. Practice, practice, practice!

Okay, so I guess my acronym is actually *Arrrp.* But my point is, the more we practice *not* letting our emotions dictate when — or even if — we accomplish something, the better we'll become at it. The second victory is easier than the first. The tenth is *way* easier than the third. And so it goes. Once you get started on the habit of not allowing negative emotions to make you procrastinate, you'll be able to succeed again and again. In this case, practice really *does* make perfect. Which is something even us imperfobiacs can appreciate.

QUARTERMASTER BRIAN TRACY'S MOST EXCELLENT BOOK

In real life, this international speaker and *New York Times* best-selling author would be the pirate captain and I'd be like, I don't know, the boatswain or powder monkey or something. But this is *my* book, which is only a little bit like real life on a pirate ship, so I'm making myself the captain and him the quartermaster. (And if ye don't think I've got the barnacles to do it, think again, ye drivel swigger!)

My point (and I *do* have one) is this: go to Amazon.com and order Mr. Tracy's book *Eat That Frog! 21 Great Ways to Stop Procrastinating and Get More Done in Less Time.*

Please really do this because, honestly, Tracy's book is brimming with practical, bite-size miracles for chronic procrastinators. Does it contain tips for time management? Sure. But Tracy's tips are good medicine for the emotional aspect of procrastination as well. In showing us how we can become "addicted" to the great feeling of accomplishment, he empowers us to deal with many of the unpleasant emotions

140

we've assigned to any given task by replacing or eclipsing those emotions with positive ones. Also, by following his strategies to tackle — and complete — even the most distasteful task first thing in the morning, we really can train ourselves to act quickly and independently of the negative feelings that keep us in bondage to unfinished business.

32. Take baby steps.

There is a reason that pretty much every motivational book ever written contains the following tried-and-true technique: it works.

Is there an unpleasant task you keep putting off? Divide it into ministeps. Is tax time looming? Today, find the phone number of your tax accountant. No, you don't have to actually call her. Just look up her number and write it in big numbers on a piece of paper on your desk. Tomorrow, go online and order the bank statements you'll need to compile your business expenses. On day three, find the receipts for any taxes you've paid, such as car tags and property taxes. On day four . . . Well, you get the idea!

So the next time you find yourself putting off an important task, shake your head and let out a grand piratey growl. Don't be shy, say, *Arrrr!* Or *Arrrp,* even.

Then get busy. Because knowing how to start — and finish — whatever goals, dreams, or changes we decide to pursue is hugely important to our success as architects and artists of our futures. Do we want to fully realize the visions we have of a better life tomorrow? Then we definitely want to learn how to finish what we start.

The Art of Change

Questions for personal reflection or group discussion:

On a scale of one to ten, how much do you struggle with procrastination? (Don't put off answering this question.) Assuming you rate higher than a two, have you figured out why you tend to put things off? What conclusions have you come to?

How has procrastination held you back? What kinds of complications or costs — emotional, relational, financial, and more — has procrastination caused in your life?

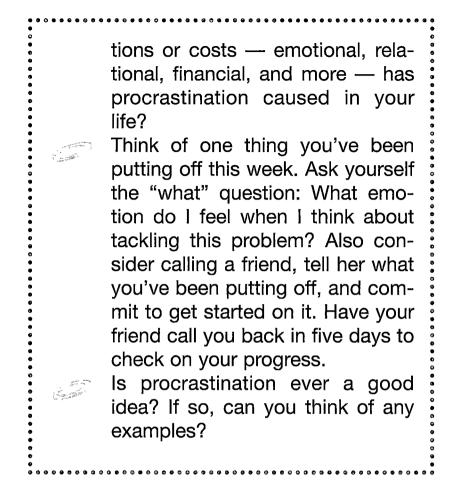

Think of one thing you've been putting off this week. Ask yourself the "what" question: What emotion do I feel when I think about tackling this problem? Also consider calling a friend, tell her what you've been putting off, and commit to get started on it. Have your friend call you back in five days to check on your progress.

Is procrastination ever a good idea? If so, can you think of any examples?

8

TRYING SOMETHING NEW WON'T KILL YOU. MOST OF THE TIME.

IF AT FIRST YOU DON'T SUCCEED, SKYDIVING IS NOT FOR YOU

Several months ago I was pumping the equivalent of a mortgage payment into the fuel tank of my SUV when I started to daydream, which is an easy thing to do when you've got forty minutes to kill at the gas pump.

I starting thinking how nice it would be to go out on a date. My former husband was just a few weeks away from getting remarried. On the other hand, in the five years since my divorce, I'd dated one guy briefly, fallen in love with someone else, and hadn't gone out with many viable candidates since.

There was a problem, and I knew what it was. The problem was that I rarely met eligible bachelors.

Maybe it's my line of work. Being a freelance writer, I don't commute to an office or have daily contact with a lot of people, which tends to limit my dating options to folks who wander down my street. Unfortunately my neighbors are all married, and the person who reads my water meter is a woman. My best bet appears to be the Federal Express guy, although I'm wondering if he's got something against brunettes. I say this because he's never, not once, hit me with the question, "What's a nice girl like you doing in a place like this?" despite the fact that I regularly call his company's 800 number and ask for a pickup. I'm a fun, congenial person, which means he's missing out on a no-fuss, drama-free dinner date. And since I believe in abstinence till marriage, it's not like I would even need the overnight service.

A MATCH MADE AT CONOCO

Still pumping gas and preoccupied with thoughts about how I never meet any eligible bachelors, I didn't immediately notice the man filling the tank of the red Suburban on the other side of the gas pump. Eventually he smiled my direction, and I made some comment about the high price of gas. He agreed, telling me what it cost him every week just to get back and forth to work.

Somewhere in the ensuing conversation about the history of oil politics and the capacity of fuel tanks manufactured overseas versus those made in America, he mentioned that he was a single dad. (Actually, I have no idea what we were talking about when he dropped the single dad gem. How could I? I was too busy pondering the fact that not even the shadow from his ball cap managed to obscure the way his eyes sparkled every time he laughed.)

My gas nozzle clicked, the rolling numbers halted, and the pump spit out my receipt. Drat. Why couldn't I have been driving a Hummer? I hear those things take *weeks* to fill.

The single dad was still talking. I had no idea about what. All I knew is that I had to say something, but since my brain wasn't registering a word he was saying, it was hard to know exactly when to interrupt.

I hadn't been up against *this* kind of problem since junior high. So I did what any composed, confident, forty-something woman would do. Holding up one hand, I blurted, "Stop. Stay. I'll be right back," and ducked back into my car. I was rummaging frantically through my purse when Kacie, who had been observing everything from the passenger seat, hissed supportively, "At least take off your sunglasses. He can't even see your eyes."

I couldn't find a pen to save my life. All I could find was lip liner. Tiramisu by Rimmel. Neutral but inviting, slightly pouty with a hint of blush. Perfect.

Returning to the gas pump, I said, "Okay, so I never do this. Like, never. But would you . . . you know . . . want to get a cup of coffee sometime with . . . um, actually . . . me?"

He grinned. "Sure."

"Unless, of course . . . I'm sorry, I didn't even ask if you're . . . you know, seeing anyone . . ."

"I'm not. I can give you my number if you want . . ."

"Oh my goodness, no. Here's my cell number." (I'd already asked him out, now I was supposed to *call* him too? I don't *think* so.) Writing my number on the back of my receipt, I heard myself rambling, "Except I couldn't find a pen . . . just my lip liner . . . and no paper . . . but if you're careful maybe it won't smudge too bad . . ."

I had to write my number twice because I kept getting the numbers wrong.

"You should probably tell me your name." He sounded amused.

"Karen."

"Nice to meet you. I'm Bean."

"Dean?"

147

"Bean."

"Are you saying Dean?"

"Bean. As in frijoles."

I had no idea why he'd been named after the inside of a burrito, but I guess truth really is stranger than fiction.

"It's a nickname," he offered. "And my little boy is Beansprout."

I gasped. "You mean, on his birth certificate?"

"Um, no. It's a nickname."

I didn't think he'd call me, but he did. That night. Turns out we have a few things in common, like faith in Jesus Christ and experience in church drama ministries. Oh, and he's got an eight-foot beanbag in his living room, just like I do. Who would have thought? Wow. Seems like a match made . . . well, if not in heaven, at least at the Conoco.

Now all I have to do is break the news to the FedEx guy. I don't think he'll be too upset. In fact, maybe I can fix him up with my water meter lady. He'll like her better anyway.

She's a blonde.

STEP — OR JOG — OUT OF YOUR COMFORT ZONE

I don't usually chat up men at the gas pump. But I'm all for trying something new — especially when I need a solution to a stubborn problem.

Although I don't do it as often as I should. Sometimes I get some sort of mental block against tackling a problem from a new direction. You've heard it said that the definition of stupidity is doing the same thing over and over and expecting different results? That's me. I've definitely done that. And I've definitely done it repeatedly in the dating department. Which is why my Conoco risk-taking moment was such a milestone. Was it comfortable? No way. Was it nerve wrangling? You bet.

And yet sometimes the best way to achieve something we've wanted for a long time and haven't been able to grasp is to embrace a new approach we haven't been willing to try. Until now.

Granted, some risks aren't worth taking. When it comes to never-before-tried strategies, sometimes there's good reason they've never been tried. So be smart. I'm also not suggesting that, when it comes to trying something new, we try anything immoral, unethical, illegal, or that takes advantage of someone else. (But I figure you already knew that.)

But too often the reason we don't try something new isn't because it's unsafe or illegal, but because it's un*comfortable.*

Look, I love comfort as much as the next person. This is why I'm picky about exercising (another nagging problem that many of us struggle to solve!). For example, I've always held the strong conviction that jogging was for *other* women. This is because when *I* jog, there are too many parts that go awry. For starters, there are always more body parts traveling up and down than forward (although I've learned a firm sports bra can help prevent black eyes and other sports injuries). Before long I'm sucking wind, my bladder's whining, and my toes have lost circulation. By the time my jog is over, my fingers have swelled up into little Jimmy Deans, and I can't remove my jogging shorts because my thighs have overheated and are now melded together.

Talk about feeling uncomfortable! This is why, whenever I need to lose a few pounds, I start walking.

Walking is the perfect alternative for people who, following their workout, still want to be able to use their bodies for other things, like moving.

Having said all that, I was walking with Kaitlyn not long ago on the Santa Fe Trail by our house when she turned to me and spoke two of the most unused words in my personal vocabulary. She said, "Let's jog."

Heaven only knows why I said yes. But I did.

I ran fifty paces before I pooped out. I know it was fifty because I counted every step. It was torture. Which is how I *know* I'm experiencing extreme short-term memory loss because, five minutes later, when Kaitlyn suggested we jog *again,* I looked at her blankly and said, "Sure."

That time I made it to one hundred.

That was six weeks ago. Yesterday I jogged two miles.

Was it comfortable? Nope. Did it work? You bet. I've dropped ten pounds and have gotten out of my fat jeans and into my pleasantly plump jeans (the skinny jeans are still fifteen pounds away). See what I mean? There's something to be said for this try-something-new approach.

33. Try something new today.
Today is the best day to try something new. Anything. For example, take a new route to work, experiment in the kitchen, or buy a new shade of lipstick. How did it work out? Were you happy with the results? If you got lost or your new shade of

lipstick makes you look fat, cheer up! Miscalculations and even failure aren't the end of the world. You're fine. You survived. In fact, you didn't "just" survive, you're learning and growing! Congratulations!

What about you? Have you been trying to create change by doing the same things you've always done? And if so, have you been frustrated by your lack of results? I hate to be the one to break it to you, but there's something peculiar about change. It requires, well . . . *change.* I know! It surprised me too!

So the first requirement to pull off real change is you need to try something new. The second thing that makes change really take root in your life is consistency.

Consistent change. Now there's an oxymoron if I ever heard one! And yet when we rise above our discomfort and do something differently than we've done it before — and do the same new thing tomorrow . . . and the next day . . . and the next — we start enjoying results. And when we get distracted or tired and *stop* doing the new thing for a season, if we rise above our discomfort *again* and embrace the new thing for one more

152

day, and then another and another and another, we can see even *more* results.

As long as we insist on comfort, we forfeit change. This is because, by its very nature, change involves discomfort. It fact, it *thrives* on it. Naturally I wish it weren't so. I wish change thrived on something a lot more pleasant, like chocolate. But it doesn't.

IT'S TIME TO TRY SOMETHING NEW. RIGHT NOW.

Why aren't you and I — on a regular basis — trying new solutions to old problems? Our love of comfort is one reason. A second reason has to do with our fear of failure. Which begs the question, why is failure so scary?

Then again, why wouldn't it be? I checked out thesaurus entries for the word *failure,* and it *is* scary. I found words and phrases like "lack of success," "nonperformance," "deterioration," "defeat," "deficiency," "downfall," "flop," and "total loss."

And if *that* weren't bad enough, how about these gems:

- born loser
- has-been
- good-for-nothing
- nobody

- might-have-been

And even this depressing pronouncement on the future:

- ne'er-do-well

No wonder no one wants to admit that they've failed or even made a mistake.

---

34. Brainstorm new approaches.
You know that change you've been longing to make? Write down ten things you haven't tried yet in your quest to get from where you are to where you want to be. Yes, ten. Get creative. Get crazy. Think outside the box. For the next ten minutes while you write, there are *no limits*. Impossible is not a workable option. I'm not saying you should *try* everything you come up with, but get your imagination going and your brain out of its box.

✺

Actually, I made a mistake recently. A series of them, in fact.

I mentioned a few pages back that I have

an eight-foot beanbag in my living room. *How,* you may be wondering, *did this come to be?* The whole thing started (as it so often does with me) on Craigslist.org. I was browsing the ads for "household items" when I spotted *exactly* what I'd never realized I'd always longed for!

It was a gigantic, eight-foot-wide beanbag.

I immediately sent an e-mail to the owner of this treasure. He called me the next morning, and we made arrangements to meet. I would have to drive forty-five minutes into Denver to pick up the beanbag, but what woman wouldn't spend a hundred dollars, two hours of her day, and forty dollars in gas for such an amazing acquisition?

The next morning, Kacie followed me to the front door with a million questions. "How long will it take you to get home with the beanbag? How big will it be? Can we keep it in my room?"

I laughed. "A couple hours, bigger than you think, and it's going in the den because we are *not* ripping out your sea cave to make room for an eight-foot beanbag no matter *how* much you beg. Which color do you think we should get?"

"Which color?"

"He's got two of 'em. Sage and khaki."

"Get *both,* Mom! Pleasepleasepleasepleaseplease!"

"Absolutely not."

Two hours later I was backing out of a Denver driveway with an eight-foot sage beanbag squeezed into the bed of my 4Runner . . . and its khaki cousin tied onto my roof.

You have no idea how big an eight-foot beanbag really is until you tie it to the roof of a car. Actually, it's about the same size *as* a car, and as I negotiated my way out of the guy's neighborhood, I laughed and thought to myself that this was not unlike driving with an SUV tied to the roof of my SUV.

I'd gone three or four blocks when I spotted flashing lights behind me. I groaned and pulled to the side of the road, running over the curb in the process. As the cop approached the car, I rolled down my window. I didn't have to ask — like they always do on TV — "What's the problem, officer?"

It was pretty obvious.

Before he could open his mouth, I addressed the problem, blurting, "Is this the most ridiculous thing you've ever seen? I knew it was going to be big, but I had *no* idea it would be *this* big! It was on Craigslist, and I wasn't even looking for anything like this, but it was a *great* deal and, honestly, how often do you find beanbags *this* size

156

and, well, what's a girl to do?"

He cleared his throat. "You seem to be having trouble driving. First you were weaving, and then you changed lanes without signaling. And just now you ran into the curb."

I thought about defending myself. Instead, I threw up my hands in agreement. "I *know* it! As you can imagine, it's kind of, well, disconcerting, what with this big thing on the roof and all! I was probably weaving because I was opening the sunroof so I can see if anything falls off — we certainly don't want *that* to happen. But I think I've got the hang of it now. Yes, I'm sure I do. No more weaving and I will *totally* remember to use my turn signal. Oh, I know what you're thinking and I agree, I should have only gotten *one* of the two, but as I was leaving the house my twelve-year-old was begging, 'Pleaseplease-please get both!' And of course you can see why she would say something like that. Don't you remember when you were twelve? Wouldn't you have found it hysterical if your mom had come home with not one but *two* eight-foot-wide beanbags? Although I have to admit that, you know, I might have gotten a *little* carried away . . ."

The officer raised one eyebrow and said dryly, "Ya think?"

Sarcasm notwithstanding, getting pulled

over wasn't so bad. In fact, he didn't even give me a ticket, although he did tell me to drive home via a rural highway instead of the freeway.

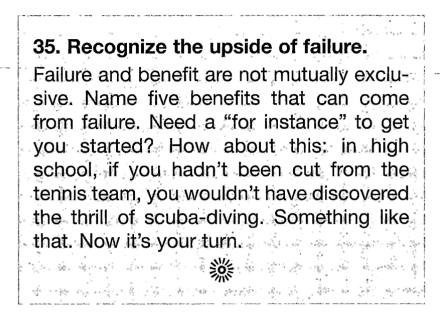

35. Recognize the upside of failure.
Failure and benefit are not mutually exclusive. Name five benefits that can come from failure. Need a "for instance" to get you started? How about this: in high school, if you hadn't been cut from the tennis team, you wouldn't have discovered the thrill of scuba-diving. Something like that. Now it's your turn.

I got the beanbags home safely, both the khaki and the sage. My daughter was thrilled and I couldn't have been happier. I think the Denver cop might even have been entertained. All that said, I don't know why people are so afraid of trying something new just because it might mean making a mistake along the way. So you might have to admit you made a little mistake. Big deal. I admitted *my* mistakes, and everything turned out all right. If you ask me, the fact that I was so willing to admit my mistake was the very reason that nice officer let me go with just a warning.

My kids disagree.

They say it's because I talked him to death.

I don't know why they say that. Don't *all* cops wrap up routine traffic stops by hurrying back to their squad cars and putting ice on their ears?

A New Look at the Bright Side

Everybody makes mistakes, fails, miscalculates, or misjudges. Admitting that it happens to us is merely stating the obvious. But we're so accustomed to thinking of failure as a negative thing that we completely miss all the great things that come with making a big mistake. Failings and mistakes are unavoidable, but fortunately they can create benefits in our lives.

Not that I'm suggesting we go out and fail *on purpose.* You and I will experience *more* than enough unplanned, unavoidable failure in our lives as it is, thankyouverymuch.

What I *am* saying is this: even as we try our best to keep failure at arm's length, we need to start recognizing the benefits that can be ours when our most carefully laid plans go awry. Failure and benefit are not mutually exclusive. They often coexist in the same world, even in the same experience.

36. Ban this phrase from your vocabulary.

The phrase is *I'm a failure.*

These words need to be banned because no matter what you have experienced or what other people may have told you, these words are simply not true. You might have experienced failure. You might have failed at a particular task. You have certainly, on occasion, gotten an outcome that was completely different from the one you'd hoped for. So call it what it is. Say, "I experienced failure." "I failed at such and such." "My results turned out different than I'd hoped."

Choose your words carefully. Use them to accurately describe an experience. Don't use them to inaccurately define you as a person. *You* are not a failure. What you are is an amazing human being committed to embracing life in all its glory and, in the process, experiencing growth and learning and, yes, even failure. (Oh, and did I mention you're also cute?)

✺

It helps to pinpoint the times when failing at something produced an impressive, totally unexpected, great outcome. When I think back on the times I've grown the most, those periods of growth were rarely prompted by success. To be sure, success is fun. It feels great. And it always teaches me something. But when I think of myself immediately after most of my successes, the word that comes to mind is *basking.* Basking is very different from striving, growing, changing, searching, grieving, processing, or wrestling. Basking is, well . . . it's sunbathing. It feels great and gives you a little vitamin D, but it's not necessarily all that productive.

Unfortunately, the stuff that leaves us deeper, richer, wiser, and stronger is that striving/growing/changing/searching/grieving/ processing/wrestling thing. And that kind of response, my friend, is more commonly prompted by failure than by success.

PERFECT CHILDREN ARE SO OVERRATED!

A couple months ago Kacie got in trouble. This is newsworthy because she is a kid who avoids trouble like the plague. She's kind and responsible. She's a self-starter. She does her homework and chores without being reminded. She's witty and quirky. (She asked for a blue streak in her hair last summer — a request I granted. It's easy to say yes to a kid you don't have to worry too much about.)

Then a couple things happened that made me realize I'd been granting her a little too much independence — despite all her grown-up behavior, she *is* still twelve. Kacie got in a little trouble, and I pulled out the Universal Parenting Standby and put her on friend-restriction for a few days.

She was devastated. With tears running down her face, she said, "But I try so *hard* to be perfect!"

This was *not* good news. I consider a concerted attempt to be perfect a much bigger problem than my daughter staying at the park too long with her friends. I needed to deal with this swiftly and intentionally.

I reached for her hand and said, "Kacie, I want you to know what I, as your mom, value and look for in your life. And it's not perfection; it's growth. I don't want a perfect daughter. Can you imagine the stress of trying to be *perfect* your entire life? How awful would that be? And even if you *could* be perfect — which of course you can't — you'd not only be stressed, you'd be shallow too! This is because a 'perfect' daughter will have learned only one lesson in life, which is how to always act like everyone wants her to act.

I'd *much* rather have an imperfect daughter who flubs up but in the process learns a thousand lessons and grows wise and rich and strong as a result."

37. Memorize this quote.
"Finish each day and be done with it. You have done what you could. Some blunders and absurdities no doubt crept in; forget them as soon as you can. Tomorrow is a new day; begin it well and serenely and with too high a spirit to be encumbered with your old nonsense."[1]

This idea was confirmed for me when I was reading a book that prompted in one chapter to write down my answer to the question, "What do you want from life?"
I scrawled my answer:

What do I want from life? Resources, choices, experiences, intimacy, love, influence, and growth. Definitely growth.
Pursuing insights, discovering and cultivating new inner territory. Being a farmer? Cultivating life for its bounty? I suppose,

but I think even more than that I want to BE the garden. I want everything that happens in my life to be like rake and hoe and plow, cultivating my heart/soul/mind so they produce and bloom and grow.

It'd be great if this kind of growth could take place in the pristine, sanitary absence of mistakes, failures, and flaws. But as luck would have it, growth almost always happens best in the presence of dirt, storms, and a good dose of fertilizer.

So what are you waiting for? Be courageous. Try something new. Step out of your comfort zone. Or jog out of it. Maybe even drive out of it. And while you're driving, if you look at your fuel gauge and see that you're nearing empty, head over to the Conoco station near my house.

Sure, gas prices are high. But I've learned that some days it's still possible to fill your gas tank to the brim and get a little change in return.

The Art of Change

Questions for personal reflection or group discussion:

- We've heard the expression *fear of failure* so often it can feel like a cliché. What do these words mean to you? What feelings rise to the surface when you think about your own past failures? How have these feelings affected your life?

- On a scale of one to ten, how open are you to trying new solutions to old problems? If you rated yourself less than seven, why?

- How can you tell whether a "new solution" is a good idea? Can you always know? If not, how can you decide whether to proceed with that idea?

- How easily can you admit when you're wrong or you've made a mistake? If it's not easy, why do you think this is the case?

- If you find it difficult to admit that you've made a mistake or failed at an endeavor, how might this impact your willingness to try new things? And if you *are* averse to trying new approaches and strategies, how does this impact your ability to pursue and attain the changes you desire? (If you can't try anything new, what's next? Do you have any sort of Plan B?)

9

ARE WE EVER REALLY ALL OUT OF OPTIONS?

THE NEXT TIME YOU COME TO THE END OF YOUR ROPE, START FLAPPING YOUR ARMS

Once upon a time there were two sisters who loved each other very much. They rarely fought. They got along really well.

They invented silly games like The Italian Hair, in which the younger sister — she was perhaps thirteen at the time — swam around in a pool with one arm sticking up out of the water imitating a "hair" (I guess you had to have been there) while the older sister lounged poolside, sunbathing and reading fashion magazines.

Life was good.

They grew up. They talked on the phone. They met for lunch at The Elephant Bar, their favorite restaurant in the world. They visited each other's homes and stayed up all night talking and doing that laugh-until-we-snort-and-need-CPR-and-diapers thing that

167

happens only between sisters or best friends.

Life was *really* good.

Then one day — I think it was a Tuesday — they entered the Twilight Zone. Or maybe alien beings invaded planet earth. Or they fell through the Looking Glass, and suddenly their worlds turned topsy-turvy. Analysts and spin doctors from seventeen different countries tried in vain to figure out exactly what happened. All anyone knew for sure is that things went terribly awry. People started asking, "What happened with those two? They used to be so close!" Whenever the sisters crossed paths, small dogs and woodland creatures ran and hid. The producer for *The Jerry Springer Show* kept both their numbers on speed dial.

Six long, bitter months went by.

For the most part, they avoided each other. The one time they tried to talk things out, it didn't go well. It went so bad, it fact, that shortly after their conversation, one sister e-mailed the other with an excerpt from a reference book titled *Proper Usage of Profanity* along with a revised version of something her sister had said. The reference book excerpt proved that it really was possible to swear *and* be grammatically correct at the very same time.

One day the oldest daughter of the older

sister said to her mother, "Don't let this turn into one of those things where, fifty years from now, the rest of us are still tiptoeing around two toothless, doddering, ninety-something sisters who can't be in the same room together."

The older sister thought about asking God for a miracle. She wondered how long she would need to pray before God would soften the heart of her sister. She figured it would take a very long time, decades even. She sighed and abandoned the idea. The next morning when she awoke, there were strange memories dancing in her head. She remembered The Italian Hair. She remembered The Elephant Bar. She remembered the sound of her sister's laugh.

Not knowing how long the nostalgic feeling would last — five minutes? seven? — or if it would ever come again, she hopped out of bed and wrote her sister an e-mail, including a script of an imaginary phone call that went something like this:

MEDIATOR: Is The Italian Hair available?

ITALIAN HAIR: Speaking.

MEDIATOR: You don't know me, but I

have a message for you from someone you used to know.

ITALIAN HAIR: Tell her to go away. I'm swimming.

MEDIATOR: Ahh, so you know who I'm talking about? You remember her?

ITALIAN HAIR: Barely. The memory's pretty foggy.

MEDIATOR: Well, try. You used to be best friends.

ITALIAN HAIR: *(Snorts.)* Yeah, well, like *that'll* happen again. NOT.

MEDIATOR: The person she used to be misses the person you used to be. Her message to you is, "Have your previous person call my previous person, and let's do lunch."

ITALIAN HAIR: No.

170

MEDIATOR: She'll buy.

ITALIAN HAIR: No.

MEDIATOR: She'll even be on time.

ITALIAN HAIR: I don't want lunch. I don't even have a mouth.

MEDIATOR: She'll order Diet Coke in a huge bowl, and you can swim around in it with one arm in the air.

ITALIAN HAIR: I'm busy. I'm washing my hair that day.

MEDIATOR: We can do this the easy way or the hard way. Don't make me get tough.

ITALIAN HAIR: Ha! Go ahead. Knock yourself out.

MEDIATOR: *Elephant Bar.*

ITALIAN HAIR: *(Long sigh.)* Okay, fine. What time?

The e-mail continued:

I can't believe I'm even writing this, but for some reason I woke up this morning and was able to actually remember the old you and me, which I haven't even been able to remember for a very long time. Do you think we could put this very ugly chapter of our lives into a sealed chamber, nuke it, sweep up the ashes, scatter them over the Baltic Sea, and call it a new day? We could say it was a season of temporary insanity when everyone was in a lot of pain and neither one of us was functioning at our best, and make a conscious decision to completely forgive, forget, and let it go. No venting, accusations, explanations, seething . . . Just nuke and scatter.

Let's get off the path to toothless, doddering, old-lady feudal drama.

I love you. I miss you. I need you. (Is this starting to sound like that song by Meat Loaf?)

I want The Italian Hair back in my life.

The older sister hit the Send button and

sighed. She didn't think anything could change. She figured even if her letter helped a little, reconciliation would still take thousands of years. Probably longer.

Several hours later, the younger sister wrote back:

In answer to your proposal . . .

ABSOLUTELY.

I have, many times, written letters to you, but I never gave them to you because it was just all so yucky and the situation was like such a buried dusty box of yuck, I figured if even a little part of that box was opened, the same ghostly angels of death that appeared at the end of *Raiders of the Lost Ark* would fly out of the box and swallow us whole, and any hint of our relationship would be lost forever.

I am very willing to put this all behind us and start over. I love you and miss you too.

Elephant Bar sounds great!

The older sister was stunned.

What had just happened? Yesterday, reconciliation was, at best, a few millennia away.

Suddenly, in the blink of an eye, Rod Serling had returned all the television sets to normal, the aliens had gone home, the world had turned right side up again.

When everything was ruined, everyone was stuck, and nothing could be done to fix a thing, something had intervened. Something had changed everything.

It was better than good.

It was bigger than great.

It was a miracle.

WHY DO PEOPLE PRACTICE SELF-HELP IN GROUPS?

I tell people that I write self-help and humor. They think I have two different careers. They don't realize I write both at the same time.

I can see their point. It *is* an unusual combination, kind of like what you might get if Dave Barry and Dr. Laura ever had kids. With each other, I mean.

I love what I do because I believe in the miracle of human potential. I believe that, deep inside, you and I have more choices, more resources, more gumption, more strength, more wisdom, and more mettle than we ever fully realize.

Recently I was asked to write a statement that would sum up my main "message," and I started to respond by writing a lengthy

174

38. Ask yourself, "So what can I do?"

Are you temporarily stuck? Ask yourself, *Okay, so what* can *I do?* If you can't do anything about one circumstance, can you do something about a different part of your problem? Can you change your perspective and/or your approach? Can you assemble a team to help you? Can you beef up your knowledge or the timetable for achieving your goal? Can you alter your attitude? What *can* you do? Answer that question, and then do it.

✺

treatise before it dawned on me that all of my books and all of my speaking can be summed up in a single sentence. And it's even a short sentence. Just three words. And they're even short words. Are you ready? Pay attention because this'll be fast:

"Yes, you can."

That's it. Nine letters, but they really do sum up the message of virtually every one of my books and seminars. Yes, you can have more joy. Yes, you can experience life without depression. Yes, you can rise above your circumstances. Yes, you can feel confident and sexy in your body. Yes, you can pursue a dream and make it come true. Yes, you can forgive the person who hurt you and finally — finally! — free yourself from the crushing responsibility of being the self-appointed keeper of the memory of all that pain.

Yes, you can imagine and then create the wonderful, happy, healthy changes you've been longing to embrace.

Yes! You can!

Except, of course . . . well . . .

Except when you can't.

I mean, let's get real. We're not gods, after all. We can't do *everything.* Sometimes things are beyond our control.

Not everything, mind you. When one thing is out of control, there's usually still something we can do. If we can't change a circumstance, we can change our perspective. If we're having a hard time changing our perspective, we can change our choices. When our choices feel limited, we can still alter our attitudes, or the ideas we welcome into our brains, or the way we spend our time. So we're never at a complete standstill, at least not in every area of our lives simultaneously.

But sometimes we come pretty close.

Sometimes there's something we need or want desperately. And for whatever reason, we can't quite reach it. We're tormented in Limbo Land where we seem unable, unwilling, or unprepared to latch onto it. And for whatever reason, we can't seem to leave it behind.

Like the two sisters in my story, we're stuck. Okay, *almost* stuck. Because even when we can't do the thing we long to do, we can always do something else.

We can ask for help.

SHHHHH. KEEP IT DOWN OR YOU'LL WAKE BIGFOOT.

In the last chapter, I mentioned the single dad I met at a gas pump at Conoco. It's time for an update. He and I had gone out twice, maybe three times, when the strangest thing happened.

Something inside me woke up. Kind of like a sleeping tiger. Or maybe like Sasquatch. All I know is that it woke up really, really hungry.

It was a fierce desire to be in a relationship. And not just any relationship. I was fiercely hungry to be in a long-term, life-partner, soul-mate, married-till-death-do-us-part kind of relationship.

This wasn't about the guy I was dating. At that point we were just getting to know each other. I wasn't falling in love with anyone, at

177

least not yet. But having someone in my life — even on a casual basis — brought back memories of the kind of hair-pulling, heart-stretching, self-sacrificing, self-nurturing, soul-warming, paradigm-busting dynamics of being in a committed relationship.

Like a cracked and crumbling dam, the wall I'd built to protect myself from those very memories gave way, and I found myself swept away in grief and longing. For the first time in five years, I wept anew over the marriage my husband and I had lost (as well as the one we'd longed for and never attained). I cried all weekend. Over the marriage that was and wasn't. Over a relationship since then that had broken my heart. Over broken dreams and unmet longings. Good thing *Old Yeller* wasn't on television that weekend; I never would have stopped blubbering!

39. Pray.

You know that change you'd love to embrace? Pray about it. Tell God about the pain, dissatisfaction, or problem that is driving you nuts. When I talk to God, sometimes I suggest ways I'd love to see my problem solved, and that's fine. But more often, I tell Him how I'm hurting and ask Him to step in and make a difference in my life however He best sees fit. And you know what? He does that very thing, and I believe He'll do it for you as well.

❀

As the last of my toppled dam was swept downstream, the final wave that flooded my world was the insatiable longing for a husband. Oh sure, I'd prayed about getting married again, but my prayers had always felt conflicted. How could I ask for a husband? Hadn't I already had one? Was remarriage God's will for me? Was it biblical? And shouldn't I strive to be content in my current circumstances? Would asking for a partner make me like a lot of women I know who are desperate to have a man in their life? Wasn't it savvier to learn to be "okay," even happy, on my own? As prayers go, mine had been tentative and conflicted, weak and predictable, latte prayers in the face of a pent-up espresso need.

But all that changed the weekend my dam burst.

After two days of solid crying, I sat on my bed hugging my knees, took a deep ragged breath, and prayed for a husband. No latte prayer this time, I found myself praying with uncharacteristic conviction. In fact, my prayer felt empowered and inspired, like God Himself had shown up and was enabling me to make this request with freedom and confidence. I prayed with an unexpected feeling of authority — not mine, but His. I found myself proclaiming, "Lord, I need a husband. Bring me a husband!"

Within two weeks, several wonderful, sincere, God-loving men appeared in my life. Whereas I'd barely met an eligible bachelor in five years, suddenly they were everywhere.

Over the next few weeks several people, unknown to each other and unsolicited by me, confided the strangest thing. They said, "I don't know why, but I've been praying that God would bring you a husband."

When I asked each one how long they'd been praying, I learned that two people had already been praying a month before *my* prayer. Another woman had been praying for me for nearly a year!

One day I e-mailed my friend Nathan: "I'm always looking to the story of Adam and Eve for clues. They were the first couple, after all. How did they find each other? Is there anything in their story that applies to us today? The only thing I've come up with so far is the fact that Eve wasn't looking for Adam. He was the one searching when God led her across his path."

Nathan e-mailed back. "Adam *had* been searching. But at the moment God brought Eve to him, Adam wasn't searching at all. He was resting. Actually, he was asleep."

I pondered his comment for the rest of the day. Could I learn something from our conversation? Unusual things had been happening ever since my God-inspired prayer. What did it all mean? Was I supposed to be like Eve, who wasn't searching but simply letting God direct her path? Was I supposed to be like Adam, resting (sleeping, actually!) while trusting God to meet his need?

I wasn't sure. All I knew was that God had heard my prayer. In fact, He'd not only heard it, He had rallied other people to make the same request months before prompting me to pray. He was *definitely* working on my behalf.

The next day I took my laptop into Borders to work. As I settled into an easy chair and turned on my computer, I noticed that two seats away a man was holding a magazine in one hand and his head in the other. Eventually, he stirred and looked up. We struck up a conversation and talked for an hour, and he left with my number. Two days later he called and invited me to dinner. How could I not say yes? After all, when I showed up at Borders, this man *had been asleep*!

In keeping with recent developments, he turned out to be a kindred soul who loves Jesus with all his heart. True love? Ahhh, not this time. As we chatted it became apparent that Curtis and I want different things for our futures. Younger than me, he hopes to one day marry and start a family. I wouldn't mind getting a pet fish.

Am I discouraged? No way.

Something about the whole experience — the surprising passion and authority of my prayer, discovering other praying people who had rallied on my behalf, the immediate appearance of eligible bachelors in my life, plus the feeling that a balm of peace had been applied liberally to my restless heart — all this has me convinced. I'm in God's hands. He's got me covered.

As for the people God brought into my life, who knows? Perhaps they're like rainbows. After my soggy weekend of tears, maybe God sent these men into my life as promises of a brighter, drier tomorrow.

But regardless of what the future holds, I'm more convinced than ever before that everything is going to be all right.

GOT CHANGE?

I don't know if you believe in God or angels or karma. Or luck or fate or pixie dust. But a lot of people do. (Believe in God, not pixie dust.) And when you talk to people about their faith, the story you'll often hear is this:

- "I was at my wit's end. And then God . . ."
- "I didn't know where else to turn. And then God . . ."
- "I'd tried everything I could think of but nothing helped. And then God . . ."

I know that everybody talks about heaven as being a really good reason to turn to God. And it is. But time and again, the reason people throw up their hands, fall on their knees, and turn to God isn't because they're longing for heaven — at least not yet — but because they're longing for *change.*

- "God, change my marriage . . ."
- "Change my kids . . ."
- "Get me out from under these stressful circumstances . . ."
- "Change these cancer cells wreaking havoc in my body . . ."
- "Heal this family . . ."
- "I haven't laughed, really laughed in

months. Can't you change my broken heart for one that's whole again?"
- "Help! I'm *so* trapped and I don't know what to do!"
- "Save me from myself . . ."
- "Rescue me out of this hurt . . ."
- "I'm so bound by bitterness I can't breathe . . ."
- "I feel lost . . ."
- "I feel angry . . ."
- "I'm so lonely . . ."
- "I feel restless and anxious, and I don't even know why . . ."
- "Change me."

This isn't late-breaking news. When Jesus walked the earth two thousand years ago, even back then people reached out to Him because they needed change. A soldier was desperate to see his servant transformed from sick to well. A woman in love with a married man was desperate for a second chance. A quartet of loyal friends longed to see a disabled friend made whole. An unscrupulous tax collector, loathed and lonely, craved fellowship with the Son of God and the hope of a better life. A thief dying on a cross longed to exchange his pain-wracked body and broken soul for a new beginning in eternity with Jesus.

HOMESICK FOR PLACES I'VE NEVER BEEN

In an earlier chapter we talked about change agents. The truth is, God is the ultimate Change Agent. Invite Him into your life and circumstances, and things can change drastically, sometimes over time, sometimes in the space of a heartbeat.

Sometimes God changes your circumstances. Sometimes He changes other people. And sometimes, when you pray, the thing that gets transformed happens to be . . . well . . . you.

Okay, you know about that rift between my sister and me . . .

Between the two of us, it turns out my sister was the "bigger" person. Even though she hadn't mailed them, she *had* been writing reconciliation letters to me long before I sent my e-mail to her.

I thought the purpose of my e-mail was to change her heart.

It wasn't.

I realize now the reason my e-mail needed to be written was to let her know God had changed *my* heart. And He did it with a prayer. On second thought, I never actually prayed. The fact is, He stepped in and changed everything based on the *thought* of a prayer. I assumed change would take decades. I was wrong. It didn't even take days. How willing was God to step in and change my world? He was so willing, He answered my prayer before I could even get the words out of my mouth.

And then there was my renewed longing to be married. Sure, I'd thought about praying about it, but I wasn't sure I should even bring it up. How willing was God to step in and change my world? He was so willing, He rallied the prayers of people who loved me. Then He prompted and empowered the prayer from me.

I believe prayer paves the way for change. But sometimes God gets a head start. Sometimes He starts paving the way before we even pray.

Take, for example, the whole thing with the cross.

Two thousand years ago, Jesus died on a cross and, as He did, He cried out, "My God, My God, why have You forsaken Me!" At that moment He was forsaken, and that abandonment was a punishment. Not for His crimes, but for ours. That punishment — that separation from God — was so horrendous that the physical manner in which it was meted out was death on the cross. Three days later Jesus was resurrected from the dead, inspiring Paul to write to the people in Corinth, "O Death, where is your sting? O

Hades, where is your victory?" (1 Corinthians 15:55).

All of that was in preparation for a single prayer that would not be uttered for a couple of millennia, if even then.

And that prayer is yours.

What is the prayer God longs to hear from you? The exact words aren't important. You can pray the words below, or you can express the same idea in your own words that are on your heart right now. Here goes:

> Jesus, thank You for loving me so much that You accepted upon Yourself a punishment that, otherwise, would have been mine. Because of what You did, I don't have to live my life and my eternity separated from God. I can have a relationship with God while I'm on earth and also later, in heaven. Your death and resurrection gave me new life; now show me how to live. In Jesus' name, amen.

Sure, you can try talking to an anonymous Higher Power, the Big Guy Upstairs, or even to The Universe. But the truth is there's a holy God who wants a personal relationship with you, who longs to know you and love you in a way that, quite frankly, "The Universe" never will. In fact, He loves you so much He sent His Son, Jesus, to pay the price for anything you've ever done, are doing today, *and* will do in the future that could stand between you and God. You're free to ask The Universe to help you when you're stuck. But for *real* change where it matters most — in your heart and soul — ask God for an intimate, life-giving relationship with Him.

What are you waiting for? Talk to God about the change you need. Maybe you need forgiveness and a new relationship with Him. Perhaps the change you long for is reconciliation in a broken relationship or new joy for yourself or even a spouse! Whatever it is, don't wait another minute. All this time you've been tentative, thinking it's up to you to broach the subject, while it's possible that your prayer is simply God's way of letting you in on what He's been preparing for you all along.

---

40. Keep track of God's activity.

Some days I can't remember what happened five minutes ago, much less six months ago. And don't even ask me what happened two years or a couple of decades ago. So why should I assume

---

that my short-circuiting brain will hang onto all the really important things, like remembering the times God has intervened in my life?

Unless you have a photographic memory (and always remember to keep it loaded with film), you might need a little help in this department too. Start a journal that is devoted to all the times God intervenes. When He makes a difference in your life — when He answers a prayer, sends a harvest moon just when you're feeling like life is mundane and boring, floods your heart with unexpected peace, causes you to cross paths with someone you needed to meet, rescues you just when you thought there was nothing that could be done — write it down. Every time God does something that shows He loves to bless you, record it in your journal.

As you fill pages with God's acts of love, your journal will be a huge encouragement any time you need to look back and be reminded that, yes, He does take care of you.

❋

And the next time you're in Colorado Springs, if you happen to run into my sister and me at The Elephant Bar, don't be a stranger. Stop by our table and say hi. We'll be easy to recognize. I look just like the picture on the back of this book, and my sister will be easy to spot as well.

She'll be the woman doing the backstroke in her Diet Coke.

The Art of Change

Questions for personal reflection or group discussion:

Who do you call for roadside assistance when you get stuck on the road of life? You long to get from where you are to where you want to be, but you seem to be spinning your wheels. Discuss the people, exercises, processes, or higher power that you turn to when you've come to the end of your own resources.

What do you think about the idea of a personal God who loves you and wants to bring good things into your life?

Have you ever turned to God when you were seeking change or needed to be healed of a physical, emotional, or spiritual hurt? Did the prayer feel like a conversation with a personal God? Did it enhance your sense that you wanted or needed a relationship with God? Or did it feel like an exercise in religion? Did you feel like He responded to you in the manner or within the time frame you had imagined?

In general, if you have reached out to God for help, what was the outcome? If you have never gone to God for help, why not?

How have your life experiences shaped your perspective on who God is and what His love is all about? If your experiences with religion have been disappointing, do you know people who claim to have had more positive experiences? Why do you think one person's experiences are so different from another's?

How do you deal with the questions or disappointments you have had with religion, faith, and God?

10

VERY FUNNY, SCOTTY. NOW BEAM UP MY CLOTHES.

I love traveling light. Not naked. Not that light. But light. Which is why I decided to go on a diet.

I made the life-altering decision a week ago, when I was browsing the "General items for sale" category on Craigslist.org and spotted this headline:

2 MONTHS OF NUTRISYSTEM MEALS FOR ONLY $300!

Realizing that was *half* the price I'd pay if I were to buy the same meals directly from the company, I got pretty excited. Still, savvy shopper that I am, I wondered if I could get an even better deal. I e-mailed the woman who was selling the food and asked if she'd take $250. She e-mailed me back and said $275 was as low as she could go. That still

193

sounded good to me!

We met in a school parking lot near my house. April was a vivacious young mom with a couple of kids in tow.

"I loved the program," she bubbled. "I had a baby six months ago and couldn't budge my last thirteen pounds of preggo-fat, so I tried this. It worked great. I know you'll love it!"

I handed her a wad of cash, and she lifted a large rectangular box from her car. There were also two smaller boxes plus a white kitchen trash bag filled with meals. We transferred everything to my car, and as I drove away, I couldn't have felt more pleased. I was not only two months away from being svelte and gorgeous, I was a certifiable bargain hound as well!

41. Weigh yourself.

Do you feel lethargic? tired? like something's weighing you down and holding you back? If you do, go ahead and identify those unwanted pounds so you can eliminate them!

Start by making a list of four or five dreams, goals, or longings that have gone

Later that evening two of my girlfriends came over. While our kids played Ping-Pong downstairs, Lisa, Ronlyn, and I drank coffee and caught up on each others' lives.

Naturally, I had to brag.

"Guess what? I'm going on NutriSystem. Bikini season, here I come! Two months from now, I'm going to be at my perfect weight. Plus, I got an amazing deal. Believe it or not, I bought two months' worth of meals on Craigslist and paid less than *half* of retail! Isn't that amazing?"

Ronlyn said, "Craigslist? Hmm. Interesting. How much did you pay?"

I beamed. "Two seventy-five."

"For two months' worth of food, right?"

"Yep."

"Who did you buy it from?"

"I don't know, some woman."

Ronlyn said, "I think I sold her that food six months ago for seventy-five dollars."

"You were on NutriSystem?" This was news to me. Then the full meaning of what she was saying hit me. I winced, "Six months ago I could have bought two months' worth of meals from you for seventy-five dollars?"

Okay, so maybe I didn't get the deal of a lifetime, but I was certain that I hadn't bought the exact same food for nearly four times the money. I pointed this out to my friend. "Ronlyn, there are half a million people in this city. There's no way we're talking about the same woman."

"But I used that same Web site to post the stuff I had for sale."

I said, "So?"

"Okay, what was the woman's name who sold you the meals?"

"April."

"That's it! That's the name of the woman I sold *my* meals to!"

I snorted. "*Lots* of women are named April."

196

Lisa chimed in. "Ronlyn, what did this woman look like?"

"I never saw her. Her husband met me with the cash, and I gave the food to him."

"See?" I said boldly. "That proves it. It's not the same person."

Call it denial, but I felt irrationally relieved. I could refrain from beating myself up for missing a deal I hadn't even known about six months earlier. But giving April a two-hundred-dollar markup on the exact same food she'd snagged from one of my closest friends for seventy-five bucks . . . Well, that would have been too much to bear!

"Let's see" — Ronlyn squinted, still trying to recall identifying details — "what else can I remember . . . Oh, her husband said she'd just had a baby."

I said weakly, "Lots of people have babies."

Halfway convinced, she shrugged. "I can't remember much else. I don't recall what kind of car he drove or anything like that. All I know is that I handed everything over in a big box, two small boxes, and a white kitchen trash bag."

Colorado Springs is a big city. But apparently it's part of a very small world.

I'm only a few days into my diet. I haven't weighed myself yet, but I know at least one thing's a lot thinner than it was a week ago. My wallet.

AERODYNAMICS CAN BE A VERY COOL THING

There's something to be said for traveling light. For example, I'm more agile when I'm at a healthy weight. I not only move faster, but the trip's a lot more enjoyable. When I'm traveling light, there's a lot less huffing and puffing going on. My joints feel better too. Plus, I'm cuter.

Sometimes I close my eyes and imagine the way I'd love to look and feel. In my mind's eye, I'm mastering difficult hikes in the Colorado sunshine with athletic ease . . . wearing a swimsuit with confidence . . . looking great in a classic little black dress . . . responding with an energetic "Yes!" when my kids ask me to play soccer with them at the park. What's keeping me from embracing all of the above? You guessed it: a couple dozen energy-zapping, confidence-sapping extra pounds. Yuck.

I have other visions too. I want to move ahead unfettered in my career. I want healthy, connected relationships with my daughters. I want the environment in my home to be uncluttered and beautiful. I want to experience a healthy, Christ-centered marriage. I want to make a difference in the lives of people I meet and in my community.

I also would love to put together a series of citywide praise and worship events. And I dream of having the financial means to do wonderful things for people. I know a married couple who are going through a rocky spell in their relationship. For two days, I've been trying to figure out how I can afford to give them a gift of a romantic weekend away from home.

42. Tell yourself you're *not* a victim.

Do you feel like a victim? Do you feel powerless to change your life? Do you want more authority over your own destiny? Authority and responsibility go hand in hand. If you want more authority, take more responsibility for your life and your future. Repeat — aloud — after me:

- I am responsible for my own problems. (Likewise, I am not responsible for other people's problems.)
- I am responsible for creating and sharpening the image I have of myself as capable and worthy.
- I am responsible for getting the skills

I need.
- I am responsible for having a plan for my life.
- I am responsible for how I interpret the circumstances and events of my life.
- I am responsible for how I respond to circumstances and events. (Likewise, I am not responsible for how other people respond to my response.)
- I am responsible for my own thoughts.

*

I can form a tremendous mental image of what I want my life to be, so what's keeping me from doing this stuff? And whatever it is, wouldn't it be great if I could drop it like the dead weight it is and start living the life I envision?

What about you? What's your story? When you think about the life you'd love to be living, what does it look like?

When you think about the kind of person you've always dreamed of being, who do you see?

When you think about aspects of your life where you feel stuck, what comes to mind?

Why can't you break out of the old and into the new?

What's holding *you* back?

Weight is visible to the naked eye. Sandbags are visible to the naked eye. Handcuffs and chains are visible too. Fears, insecurities, old wounds, painful memories, financial irresponsibility, procrastination, grudges, pride . . . These things might be invisible but, like anchors planted firmly on the floor of an otherwise inviting bay, they hold us back from getting where we want to be.

MAYDAY! MAYDAY!

Dumping the stuff that's holding us back isn't just about progress. Sometimes it's about survival. Like a spaceship in crisis, we're losing power fast, and if we don't start jettisoning the unnecessary weight and burdensome baggage slowing us down, there's a good chance we're going to crash and burn.

I know a woman who ate her way into a size twenty-four and stayed there. One day we were talking about regrets, and she confessed, "There's something I've never told anyone. I know that if I could ever forgive myself for this one thing, it would be the moment I could stop punishing myself with

201

food." What baggage does she need to jettison if she's going to pull out of the tailspin she's in? Shame comes to mind, as does unforgiveness.

Another woman can't seem to break up with her loser boyfriend. When asked why she always goes back to him, she confessed, "I was molested as a child. Whenever I date a guy who's got it together, the thought of one day telling him what happened to me freaks me out. My fear is that healthy guys with great childhoods won't be able to handle my story, that they'll be so shocked they'll reject me. The guy I'm with now? He doesn't treat me all that good, but he's had a rough life too, so at least he's not shocked by what happened to me."

If this woman is going to stop bouncing around in turbulent airspace and learn how to soar, what excess baggage needs to go? How about the fear of rejection? Or memories that, twenty years after the tragic events that spawned them, are keeping her chained to additional abuse and pain?

Letting go of the baggage that keeps us mired in pain or frustration might sound like a no-brainer, but the truth is that it requires some intention and thought.

How do we do it? Where do we begin?

1. Let go of the excuse that unpleasant people or circumstances are holding you back.

What's holding you back? Is it a person who is part of your life? Someone who is critical or controlling, unpredictable or irresponsible? A boss, perhaps? Or a husband or parent? Maybe it's the memory of people who *used* to be in your life. You haven't seen them for years, but something they said or did still defines you.

Or it could be circumstances — like illness or financial stress — that are a reality right now in your life. Even memories of past circumstances — childhood poverty, growing up with an alcoholic parent, betrayal experienced in a marriage that ended years ago — can trip you up, can't they?

And yet . . .

Not everybody believes that people or circumstances have to trip us up, weigh us down, or hold us back. Some folks believe that the only thing that can hold us back is, well . . . the person we see in the mirror every morning.

Viktor Frankl, a Viennese psychiatrist and concentration-camp survivor, became convinced that nothing — not even the most brutal circumstance or abuser — need hold us back from growth, change, and triumph.

Seems like an outrageous claim, doesn't it? Yet Frankl, after surviving three years of starvation and brutality at the hands of the Nazis, wrote these words: "Even the helpless victim of a hopeless situation, facing a fate he cannot change, may rise above himself, may grow beyond himself, and by so doing change himself. He may turn a personal tragedy into a triumph."[1]

43. Decide, starting today, that you won't be held back.

We've all met or read about people who, even in the middle of dire circumstances and under the control of tyrannical authority figures, weren't held back. They still grew personally, stayed emotionally healthy, hung onto hope and dreams. They stayed large and vibrant — inside — even if an event or person was temporarily causing them pain or limiting their freedom.

Likewise, we all know people who, regardless of the positive or negative nature of the people or circumstances in their lives, stay small, limited, and held back.

Events and people don't hold us back as much as the power we give to those events and people. People don't exercise control over you; you *give* them control. As you picture the life you want, decide that from now on you won't allow outside forces to hold you back.

❄

Chris Gardner is a survivor of a different sort.

Following a violent childhood, Chris found himself jobless and homeless as a young man. In a bold move, he convinced a brokerage firm to accept him for training. Wearing a borrowed suit and sleeping at a flophouse — or when no one was looking, spending nights under his desk at Dean Witter — Chris began making cold calls and studying to pass the test to become a stockbroker.

This was challenging enough. Then Chris's ex-girlfriend showed up at the flophouse where he sometimes slept, handed him their twenty-month-old son, and walked away. For the next year Chris lived a surreal double life: Weekdays, he dropped his son off at day care and then walked to work. Evenings and weekends, they roamed the streets of San Francisco, homeless.

Housing costs — and the time necessary to build a client base — meant Chris could barely afford day care, food, and a small amount of savings. Sometimes they slept at a homeless hotel, sometimes public bathrooms.

Chris could have given up. Instead, dire circumstances drove him forward:

> A taunting voice that had lurked in the back of my mind now seemed to suddenly gather strength. . . . The voice mocked me, sounding a hell of a lot like [my stepfather] Freddie, just telling me . . . *Who do you think you are? . . .* The voice made me angry and made me fight harder. Who did I think I was? I was Chris Gardner, father of a son who deserved better than what my daddy could do for me, son of Bettye Jean Gardner, who said that if I wanted to win, I could win. . . . Whatever more I had to do, whatever burden I had to carry, I was going to rise up and overcome.[2]

Today Chris Gardner is a successful stockbroker and the founder of Gardner Rich & Co., a multimillion-dollar brokerage firm. You may have seen the movie *The Pursuit of Happyness,* based on his book of the same name.

44. Show your emotions who's boss.

The next time you feel like quitting, do the unexpected. Show yourself who's boss by doing something other than what you feel like doing. My dad knew a man who, wanting to lose weight, showed his hunger who was boss by sitting down at every meal and refusing to touch his food for *ten minutes.* Author and speaker Matthew Kelly practices sitting completely still for long periods of time, rising above the urges to move, scratch his nose, or stretch his legs.

One morning I felt like sleeping in, so I drove to a hiking trail instead. On the trail, when I felt like quitting, I kept walking. When I felt like walking, I jogged a little.

The next time you feel like quitting, don't! Try one of these ideas instead: (1) keep doing what you're doing; (2) do what you're doing, only harder; or (3) do something completely different that still takes you in the direction you want to go! Just don't stop!

I read his book a couple nights ago. I started it as I was crawling into bed at eleven and finished it around 5:00 a.m. At five in the morning, you'd think I'd have been dog-tired. Instead, I felt inspired. If Chris could rise above circumstances *that* dire, what was I complaining about? I got up, washed the dishes on my kitchen counter, straightened my desk, opened my laptop, and got busy writing.

Matthew Kelly, in one of my favorite books, has this to say on the subject:

> Everything is a choice. This is life's greatest truth and its hardest lesson. It is a great truth because it reminds us of our power. Not power over others, but the often untapped power to be ourselves and to live the life we have imagined.
>
> Most people never fully accept this truth. They spend their lives arguing for their weaknesses, complaining about their lot in life, or blaming other people for their weaknesses and their lot in life. . . .
>
> Some may say that we do not choose our circumstances. You'd be surprised. We have much more power over the circumstances of our lives than most men and women would ever admit. And even if circumstances are thrust upon us, we

choose how we respond to those circumstances.[3]

He concludes that "the day we accept that we have chosen to choose our choices is the day we cast off the shackles of victimhood and are set free to pursue the lives we were born to live."[4]

What's holding me back from making my dreams come true? I'm realizing it's not a *what* but a *who,* and the *who* is me.

Who's holding *you* back?

2. Letting go is a choice. You don't have to do it . . . but why wouldn't you?

One day Kacie got her feelings hurt. An adult family friend had unknowingly teased her about something she was sensitive about, and she was in tears.

How was I going to walk her through this? How could I help her let go of the hurt?

She was all of about nine at the time. We had just driven home from meeting friends — including the friend who had teased her — for ice cream, and she had cried most of the way home. She was still teary-eyed as we pulled into the driveway.

It was a beautiful starry night. I shut off the engine and opened the sunroof. We flung our heads back and watched the stars awhile before speaking. For more than an hour we sat together, talking and figuring it all out. At one point I said, "Kacie, someone hurt your feelings. Bruised or otherwise, those feelings are yours, they belong to you, and you can hang on to them for as long as you want. For the rest of your life if you want to."

She looked surprised. This wasn't what she expected to hear. She was expecting something about forgiving and forgetting, not hanging on forever.

I added, "But I want you to know what those broken feelings would look like if you could see them with your eyes. They're tiny pieces of glass, just like if someone took something of yours — a crystal vase maybe — and dropped it on a concrete floor. And now there are all these sharp pieces and shards. But they're *your* shards. And if you want to scoop up the pieces and clutch them tightly in your hands, you certainly can. If you decide to hold on to them, no one can wrestle them from you. Not me, not your dad, not a boyfriend, not a pastor, not even a counselor. But the longer you hang on, the more they'll cut you. In fact, every day you clutch stubbornly to those razor-sharp pieces of broken glass, the more you'll bleed.

"Now, like I said, they're yours. You can do with them what you want. But I'm hoping you'll make the choice to let them go. Just open your hands, and let them go so they can't keep cutting you, so you don't use them to keep wounding yourself over and over again."

She got it. She really did. To this day, when someone hurts her feelings or mine, we talk about the broken glass and how we can choose either to hang on or let go. Letting go doesn't mean that what happened was okay. And it doesn't mean we're in denial or that our feelings aren't important.

On the contrary, letting go simply means we're taking responsibility for our own well-being, that we're making the choice not to prolong the pain.

Life inflicts enough pain, don't you think? Why in the world do we want to clutch all that brokenness to our bosoms, adding self-inflicted wounds that can be deeper and bloodier than the original hurt?

Has someone or something left you clutching a handful of broken glass? Has your past left you with feelings of powerlessness, shame, inferiority, hopelessness, or rejection? Are you dogged by anxiety or fears? If so, open your fists.

3. Picture it gone.

I love images. Don't you? Imagining something that's painful and then picturing something you can do to keep it from causing further wounds is a powerful exercise.

Like the image of broken glass. Imagining broken glass — and picturing myself either clutching the pieces tightly or watching them fall out of my open hands — has helped me on countless occasions.

There are other images, too, that can help us let go, whether the thing we need to release is a hurt feeling or a fear or the belief that we don't deserve anything better in life than what we currently are experiencing.

Here are a couple more ideas.

Imagine a bathtub. Imagine yourself pulling the stopper out of the drain. Imagine the water swirling above the drain as it leaves the tub. Now think of whatever has been holding you back — fears, anxieties, myths of a glass ceiling — and feel it draining out of your brain, your body, and your life.

---

45. Out with the bad, in with God.

Paul writes in Philippians 4:13: "I can do all things through Christ who strengthens me."

Take a deep breath. As you do, imagine yourself inhaling the very presence and

---

You can also imagine suitcases. A lot of them. You've got one in each hand, another under your arm, one hung by a long strap over your shoulder. You're wearing a heavy backpack too. You're in an airport, struggling down a long corridor, sweating, loaded down, scurrying to catch the flight that will take you somewhere wonderful. Perhaps this plane will fly you to a tropical paradise, or to a bright new city where opportunity glistens, or into the arms of someone you love. You hear a voice on a loudspeaker, announcing the final boarding call. You try to run. As you do, the heaviest bag keeps crashing painfully into your left thigh. You feel a strain and burning muscles in your back and shoulders from the weight of the bags. Your face is hot and sweaty. At this rate, there's no way you'll make your flight.

Now imagine yourself dropping the suitcases. Hear the thuds as they drop onto the floor. You also sling off the shoulder bag and wriggle out of the backpack. Imagine the freedom! Laughing, you start to run. You feel free. Your body feels light and fast. Unencumbered, you sprint to the gate. The flight attendant takes your boarding pass and smiles. "I'm glad you made it," she says. You grin and say, "Not nearly as glad as I am!"

What picture can you think of that represents the freedom you long to experience? Come up with something that paints a picture of . . .

- letting go
- moving on
- traveling light

Picture it. Then live it.

4. Let it go into the strong hands of Someone bigger than you.

For several months I'd been feeling fatigued and stifled. I was having a hard time meeting my writing deadlines. I was feeling sad and hopeless in my personal life as well. To make matters worse, it seemed as though everywhere I looked, people I loved — including my sisters and my daughters — were hurting over circumstances in their lives. If I could use a single phrase to describe what was plaguing me, it was a profound sense of sorrow.

One Sunday I visited my parents' church to hear guest speaker Larry Lea. In 1986, Lea authored the best-selling book *Could You Not Tarry One Hour?* and was pastoring a five-thousand-member church in Rockwall, Texas. Not long after that, controversy arose over Lea's fund-raising and management. A year later, an independent audit cleared him of all the allegations that had been made against him. Nevertheless, it was a very stressful, painful season in his life.

More than a decade later, Lea is once again living his passion, traveling, writing, and preaching. The Sunday morning I heard him, he talked about sorrows. As I listened, two things came to mind: I knew this guy was speaking from personal experience, and I knew he was speaking to me.

And here's what I heard him saying: When sorrows are holding us back, we can do one of two things. We can hang on to those sorrows, or we can present them, like sacrifices, to God, letting Him take those sorrows and resurrect them as new life and new hope.

Sacrifice and resurrection are important themes in the Bible. In Old Testament days, people sacrificed livestock to God. The animals were killed, then consumed by fire. In return, God forgave the people for wrongdoing in their lives. For thousands of years, sacrifice and new beginnings went hand in hand.

Two thousand years ago, God orchestrated another altar, another gift, another sacrifice — with a few key differences. This time, the sacrifice didn't involve fire, but it did involve death. The altar wasn't shaped like a table but like a cross. And the gift wasn't a lamb but a man named Jesus. But the most distinguishing feature of this sacrifice was that, this time, the sacrifice didn't stay dead. Three days after He was killed, Jesus was resurrected.

With this crucial twist to an old story, God's message became clear: "If you're willing to accept this sacrifice on your behalf, I'll not only forgive you for everything you have done wrong, I'll resurrect *you* into new life. I know you've felt dead and hopeless, but I've made it possible for you — through the death and resurrection of My Son, Jesus — to experience new life and new hope instead."

46. Have some faith!
Faith is the substance of things hoped for and the evidence of things not yet seen.[5]

Think of ten goals or dreams you want to see come true in the next five years. Now write them down in the present tense *as if they are already true*. For example:

I am at a healthy weight, and I love my body!

I make $100,000 a year.

My home is beautiful and uncluttered.

I am investing in the lives of people around me.

My marriage is healthy and happy.

I am no longer being held hostage by painful memories or unforgiveness.

You get the idea. Now get started!

1.
2.
3.
4.
5.
6.
7.
8.
9.
10.

When Larry Lea told everyone to lay their sorrows on the altar and let God resurrect those dead, hopeless sorrows into new life and joy, the idea made sense to me. A lot of sense.

At the end of the service, many people stood and made their way to the front of the church for prayer. Others left money in a small wicker basket on the pulpit. It wasn't a burning altar, and there were no livestock involved, but with their offerings these folks were saying, "Here are my sorrows. I'm leaving them on the altar, Lord. Resurrect them into something beautiful."

I was tired of feeling draggy and held back. I was tired of feeling sad and hopeless. I was tired of feeling, yes, *sorrowful.* I wanted to leave it all on the altar.

I didn't have money. Instead, I found a piece of paper and wrote on it the first names of my sisters and daughters. I wanted the sorrows in their lives to be turned into joy.

I also knew that there were sorrows — certain fears, emotions, failures — related to my career that were holding me back. Writing is such a personal endeavor, there are a million emotions that can trip up the process. And it doesn't happen just to me. Writers tormented with writer's block are common enough to be a cliché. There's a quote by Ernest Hemingway that has given me a lot of comfort through the years. Alluding to his own fears and demons, he wrote, "I would stand and look out over the roofs of Paris and think, 'Do not worry. You have always written before and you will write now. All you have to do is write one true sentence. Write the truest sentence you know.' "[6]

When it came to my writing, I was tired of being held back. I was tired of writer's block, angst, and fears. I longed for renewed energy, unfettered focus, and new creativity.

In the bag at my feet, I happened to have a copy of one of my books. I pulled it out and walked discreetly to the front of the church. A lot of people were standing and walking around, so I didn't draw any attention as I slipped my book into the offering basket with the note of the names of four women I love.

For a moment I wondered what the pastor would think when, among the checks and bills, he discovered a list of names and a book. Then I smiled. It didn't matter. God knew what those items stood for. He knew intimately the sorrows I was putting to rest on the altar.

He knew I was letting go.

Traveling light is a good way to travel. Sometimes it's the *only* way to get from where you are to where you want to be.

I don't know what you need to jettison to make it happen. Which is okay, because *you* know. So get busy! Dump your excuses. Let go of your shards of broken glass. Picture yourself flinging off baggage and running free. Figuratively and even literally, place your sorrows on the altar and ask God to resurrect them into something beautiful and healthy and alive.

And if the thing you need to shed happens to be a few pounds, go to Craigslist.org and look for my ad. I hate to part with my Nutri-System meals, but I can't afford not to.

Based on April's profits, at the rate this stuff keeps appreciating, if I sell now I can put one of my kids through college.

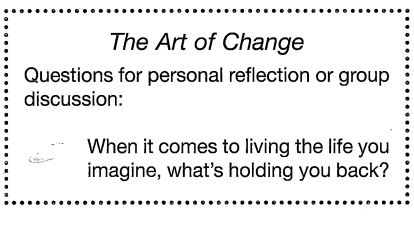

The Art of Change

Questions for personal reflection or group discussion:

When it comes to living the life you imagine, what's holding you back?

Do you feel as if outside forces or people are standing in your way? Are there things you need to shed in order to get from where you are to where you want to be?

Of the illustrations presented in this chapter — letting go of broken glass, draining a bathtub, dropping heavy luggage and running free — which one meant the most to you, and why?

Bitterness can be one of the hardest things to let go of. What experiences have you had with unforgiveness? If you've been successful at forgiving others and letting go of bitterness, how did you do it? If you haven't been successful and there is someone you need to forgive, name something you can do today that will take you one step closer to the freedom you crave.

Are you hanging on to a belief about yourself that is holding you back? If so, what is that belief? How did you come to embrace it? As you think about it in a new light, what makes you think it is false or harmful? Name something you can do today that will help you let go of that belief or replace it with a healthier belief.

11

GOT OBSTACLES? NEVER MIND.
SILLY QUESTION.

IF EVERYTHING'S COMING YOUR WAY, YOU'RE IN THE WRONG LANE

It had been a long day for Renee. Not only had she been on the road for an hour collecting her kids from various after-school activities, she had just negotiated her Montero through a horrendous hailstorm to reach the middle school where the last child awaited her arrival.

Hunter tossed his backpack into the backseat and climbed in, talking excitedly about the storm that had swept the campus twenty minutes earlier. The rest of the drive home, the conversation focused on the hail, some of which had been the size of small kitchen appliances. Renee was enjoying the lively chatter when, all of a sudden, she jerked the car toward the curb, slammed on the brakes, and began to scream.

"I don't believe this! I can see them!

They're everywhere!"

Sixteen-year-old Connor gripped the dashboard. "What is it?" he asked, heart racing. "What do you see?"

"Can't you see them?" Renee shrieked. "They're everywhere! They're *huge!*"

By now Hunter and Isaac, thirteen and ten respectively, were climbing over the front seat to peer through the windshield. All three boys continued staring outside as their mother screamed and pointed.

They couldn't see a thing.

Their mother was practically sobbing.

They stared again. Was she seeing ghosts? aliens? Was she hallucinating? Had she developed some sort of Bruce Willis–like sixth sense? Had she gone *insane?* Renee pointed and choked out the words, "There! Right *there!* Hundreds of them!"

The boys looked but saw no ghosts or little green men. Their mother had definitely gone off the deep end.

"All over the hood!" Renee shrieked in frustration. *"Hail dents!"*

Sure enough, the glassy-smooth finish of Renee's beloved Montero had enough dents to land a starring role in an Allstate commercial.

The hailstorm had taken its toll. The good news was that Renee wasn't destined for the front page of the *Weekly World News.* Although if she *had* made the cover, can you imagine the headline?

Soccer Mom Sues Aliens for Bodywork

Weird things come at us when we're on the road, and it doesn't matter if we're carpooling to a son's middle school or traveling down the road of life. The problem is, we don't *want* obstacles and dings and danger. We don't *want* hail dents on our hoods and bug juice on our windshields. We want good stuff coming at us, *only* good stuff, and plenty of it.

Unfortunately, that's never going to happen. And if we ever *do* find ourselves in a situation where everything's coming our way, it probably means we're in the wrong lane.

Dents, Bugs, and Potholes: You Can't Leave Home Without 'Em

There are some changes I'd love to make in my life. I mentioned two of them at the beginning of this book:

- Settle into a committed, long-term relationship with my skinny jeans instead of having all these short-lived flings.
- Fall madly in love.

225

Don't quote me as saying that getting the flu is a great way to jump-start weight loss, but that's pretty much what happened to me a couple of months ago. I started feeling queasy on Christmas Day. By that night, I was shivering beneath layers of blankets, leaving my little fever-nest every hour or so to kneel on the cold bathroom tile and empty my guts.

The bad news is that this went on for three days.

The great news is that I lost six pounds.

47. Write on your bathroom mirror.

I don't care if you use sticky notes, dry-erase marker, or lip liner, just get this message on your bathroom mirror where you'll see it first thing every morning: "I am better equipped to tackle problems than I've been in my entire life. In fact, I have never been a more worthy adversary to any and all adversity than I am today, at this very moment."

By New Year's Eve, I was feeling much better, although still a little weak. I'd been invited to a New Year's Eve party at a friend's house, and I wondered if I felt well enough to go. I came *this* close to staying home, but at the last minute I put on my best party face and a really great pair of black, spike-heeled boots and drove to Gaylyn's place.

By nine o' clock, several dozen friends were mingling and laughing around tables loaded with platters of wings and chips and fruit. Someone turned up the music, and several couples started an impromptu dance in the dining room.

When a newcomer walked in the front door carrying a plate of cookies, I thought he looked a little lost. Oh, he looked tough enough — leather jacket, cowboy boots, and a semiconfident grin — but still a little lost.

Since I can get shy around guys I'm attracted to, my first inclination was to steer clear of this one. Then I shook off the thought and chided myself for being such a baby. *Just treat him like any other guy you're* totally *not attracted to,* I told myself and walked up and introduced myself.

Eric and I talked the rest of the night. I imagine we would have seen the New Year in together if he hadn't pulled out his keys and prepared to leave around eleven. He said he had to get home so he could let his dog out. He didn't ask for my number; I didn't offer.

He called the next morning, confessing

that it had taken him a while to figure out how to get my home number. He also admitted that letting his dog out had been an excuse.

"Look, I've been divorced all of three months. I haven't dated in years. This is really new to me, and I needed time to think." I laughed at his honest confession and said yes when he invited me to meet him for coffee. We spent most of that day together, talked every day on the phone for the next five days, then spent most of the following weekend together.

By Sunday afternoon, we were drinking coffee and bumping knees at a little table at Barnes and Noble when Eric told me his head was still spinning from his divorce and that he probably wasn't ready for a relationship. We agreed to keep our new friendship at just that — a friendship — and nix any thoughts of dating for a while.

We didn't talk for a week. The following Sunday, I saw him at church. After having lunch with mutual friends, we escaped to spend the rest of the afternoon drinking coffee and talking at a local Starbucks. When he walked me to my car and kissed me in the parking lot, it seemed like the most natural development in the world, and suddenly "not dating" seemed like a conversation from about four lifetimes ago.

When it comes to losing weight, the only thing better than the flu is a severe case of infatuation. In no time, I'd dropped ten more pounds and gained one hundred seventy. Eric was quickly becoming a very pleasant addition to my life. He brought flowers. He brought cookies and kisses. He even washed dishes. And what that man could do with a back rub should have required a license to thrill.

A week before Valentine's Day he showed up with music. We danced in the kitchen to one of his favorite CDs, to a song we decided could be ours and ours alone.

Two days later it was over. He wasn't ready. It was too fast. He was only four and a half months divorced and his head was still spinning and he needed more time.

Honestly, I don't blame him. Four months after my marriage ended, I wasn't ready for a relationship either. But I'm not newly divorced anymore. My marriage ended five years ago. My ex has remarried. I'm ready to move on. Not to mention that a couple of years ago, I got my heart broken. I wrote about it in my book *Due to Rising Energy Costs, the Light at the End of the Tunnel Has Been Turned Off.* If you've read that book, you might remember I refer to this particular man as Skippy. It's not his real name, of course. He actually has a very nice name. But without meaning to, we'd managed to hurt each other, and I was still smarting when I wrote the book. Calling him Skippy seemed like such small revenge in light of such a very big hurt. In fact, I thought the hurt would never end. It finally did, although it took an entire year. (Many of the techniques in *Due to Rising Energy Costs* were my own desperate strategies to rise above that pain.) But eventually the pain subsided and my joy returned, and seven months later I went to that New Year's Eve party and met Eric.

My point is that, at that moment, I was *so* ready for something new, something wonderful, something that would last.

Oh well. Two out of three ain't bad.

CAN YOU SAY "SETBACK"?

After things ended with Eric, I felt a lot of things. Like, you know, hunger. Not *true* hunger, but the kind that makes you regain ten pounds in about six hours due, as I'm sure you can understand, to the liberal therapeutic application of ice cream and Eggo waffles.

The other thing I experienced was dread. I was feeling a little numb at the time (it might have been the disappointment, but it was more likely all those carbs), and I remember thinking, *Wow, I hope this doesn't hurt in a day or two. I really don't want to go through that kind of pain again.*

I was, of course, remembering my breakup with Skippy, remembering the dark alchemy of loss, remembering months of hurt.

Now, granted, the impact of the end of a five-week dating thing is different from the impact of the end of a twelve-month madly-in-love thing, but I'd suspected that Eric and I had potential, so I was disappointed. Plus, I was pain-shy, and the thought of another broken heart — even if it was a *much* smaller crack, a hairline fracture, really — wasn't something I was looking forward to.

48. Read a really great book.
Pick up a copy of *The Adversity Advantage: Turning Everyday Struggles into Everyday Greatness* by Paul G. Stoltz and Erik Weihenmayer. Or this one: *Man's Search for Meaning* by Viktor E. Frankl. Or this one: *The Pursuit of Happyness* by Chris Gardner. Or this one: *Boogers Are My Beat* by Dave Barry.

Okay, just kidding about the booger book. Although if you read it and see how it can be loosely interpreted as dealing in any way, shape, or form with adversity, e-mail me and let me know. I'm a huge fan of Dave's, and if I can prove to the IRS that his book has *anything* to do with the content of this chapter, I can buy my own copy and claim it as a tax deduction.

❋

But here's what I discovered. The strategies that I'd wrestled so desperately to acquire and practice when my relationship ended with Skippy, well, they came a lot easier this time. And I didn't need a year to nurse my disappointment before moving on. I needed a couple of weeks. Turns out I really did learn some lessons last time around about how to regroup, patch up, and heal up.

What do you do when you experience a setback?

A lot of people, when they get clobbered by an obstacle, walk away chanting this mantra: "From this moment forward, I'm going to avoid *every* situation where I might possibly get clobbered." Other people draw this conclusion instead: "I'm going to *try* to avoid getting clobbered, but if and when it happens, it's not the end of the world. I *will* survive, plus I'll gain even greater wisdom on how to regroup, patch up, heal up, and get back in the game."

If we think of it in football terms, what would happen if a wide receiver got clobbered just before he got into the end zone — and decided to do everything he could to stay out of the end zone from that point on? He would be worthless to his coach, teammates, fans, and even himself.

Like that soon-to-be-unemployed wide receiver, you and I can work hard to stay out of the end zone, or we can get back in the game of life a little wiser and a little more prepared. I'm convinced a great goal is to come away from every setback — not more gun-shy or broken — but stronger, wiser, and with a better stocked first-aid kit so the *next* time a play doesn't go as planned and we end up on the bottom of the pile, we know just what to do to climb out of the disappointment and get back in the game.

IS THERE AN OBSTACOLOGIST IN THE HOUSE?

What do you and I really know about setbacks, adversity, and obstacles? Figuring I could use a little tutoring on the subject, I went to the Yellow Pages and looked up "obstacologist." After all, everyone I know whines about obstacles. I figure there's got to be somebody making a living studying these things.

Turns out there's no such thing as an obstacologist. At least not officially. Although I did come across a book titled *The Adversity Advantage* coauthored by Paul Stoltz, a bestselling author on adversity, and Erik Weihenmayer, a world-class adventurer and athlete who has climbed the tallest peak on every continent despite the fact that he has been blind since his early teens.

In the first chapter the authors ask, "What if, as a result of completing this book, you could use any, and I mean *any,* adversity to your advantage? What if you could convert your everyday struggles, big and small, into the kind of fuel that powers you past everyday normality to everyday greatness?"[1] Adversity as fuel. Now *there's* a concept. Imagine! You would certainly never experience any shortage of raw material. In fact, the whole idea makes me think of the article I read recently about a man who figured out how to power his car using pond scum. (No, really, it's true. Google it!) My point is, there's something intriguing about taking a substance as common and unsought-after as pond scum and turning it into a valuable commodity. What if you and I could do the same thing? What if we could take something as common and despised as adversity and use it to our advantage? If we would take our problems and use them as fuel to get wherever we want to go?

I'll be honest. When I hit a bump in the road (or hail on my hood, crack in my heart, or scum in my pond) my first thought isn't, *Oh goody! Here's something I can really use!* And my first emotions aren't exhilaration, gratitude, or anticipation. Actually, when adversity strikes, my emotions lean more toward dread, fear, and resignation.

USING ADVERSITY TO YOUR ADVANTAGE

So how do we do it? How can we choose to *use* adversity to our advantage, instead of giving it permission to drop-kick our butts? Here are six approaches that have worked for me and for other people as well.

1. "I am stronger, smarter, and better equipped than I've ever been."

As I just mentioned, when adversity strikes, my emotions lean toward dread, fear, and resignation. At some point, I have to make a conscious choice to redirect my thoughts and emotions down a healthy, positive path. I'll admit, this is rarely my first response, and it never feels as natural to me as, say, moaning and whining. But it always serves me better in the long run. Plus, the quicker and more frequently I choose this healthy, positive path, the more natural it feels.

Here are some of the healthier, positive thoughts I make a conscious effort to embrace:

> I'm not the same person I was the last time I faced adversity. This time, I'm stronger and smarter. I have more resources. I am better equipped to tackle this problem than I've been in my entire life. In fact, I have never been a more worthy adversary to my adversity than I am today, at this very moment in time.

When asked what he would do differently if he had the chance, entrepreneur Gordon Stewart couldn't think of anything. He said, "I don't think there's anything different to do because everything is a learning curve. Yes, we made mistakes in the past, but we paid the price and we fixed it."[2] Stewart started his first business — an air conditioner distributorship — at the age of twenty-six. He went on to start other successful businesses, including a daily newspaper. Most recently, he helped turn one rundown hotel into Sandals, the largest and most luxurious resort chain in the Caribbean. Obviously his attitude that "everything is a learning curve" continues to reap impressive rewards in his life.

I love the "everything is a learning curve" attitude. After all, the human brain processes more than sixty thousand thoughts per day. Whether we realize it or not, you and I are in a constant mode of processing and learning. We couldn't *not* be smarter than we were yesterday even if we tried.

Another way to look at adversity is like it's a good, demanding workout. If you ask me, adversity can do for our inner resources what weightlifting does for our muscles.

Remember the *last* time you faced an obstacle? Whether you rose to the occasion and triumphed, or whether you experienced defeat, there was a struggle, wasn't there? You might think the story ended there, with victory or defeat, but it didn't. Think of lifting weights at the gym. You struggle and sweat. Maybe you manage to complete all fifteen repetitions, or maybe your muscles fatigue and you stop after eleven, unable to lift that dumbbell one more time. You rack your weights, but the story doesn't end there, does it? You go home. You rest. And while you rest, your body is repairing and rebuilding muscle tissue until it's stronger than it was before. The next time you show up at the gym and face those weights, you're better equipped. *Even if the last time you got tired and quit,* you're actually stronger now than you were then.

---

49. Create your own adversity-buster résumé.

Imagine you are applying for the job of Adversity Buster. Why are you qualified for this position? What past experience do you have taking on adversity and coming out on top? What successes have you had? When you've failed, what strengths and wisdom did you gain in the process? Write it like a real résumé, with categories such as objectives, strengths, job experience, areas of expertise, personal attributes, education, and even references.

❋

Our brains never stop sorting information and solving problems, even while we sleep. Likewise, after you faced your last adversity, your mind and spirit kept sorting and solving even as you rested and regrouped. The result? Whether or not you recognize it, admit it, or take advantage of it, your problem-solving resources — including wisdom, intellect, optimism, imagination, and more — are stronger than they were the last time you exercised them.

The next time you face adversity, speak the following statement (and listen to yourself):

> It doesn't matter if I triumphed over my last adversity or not. Just the fact that I took it on has left me better equipped than I used to be, with greater inner resources that I can apply to whatever challenge I'm facing today. In taking on this present problem, I will discover and develop even more strength and strategies, leaving me even better equipped to triumph over new obstacles in my future.

Friedrich Nietzsche said it well: "Whatever does not destroy me makes me stronger."

2. "This is *such* a piece of cake!"

Kacie taught me a really cool principle about facing adversity. To make matters more interesting, she was probably all of eight when she did it.

She had been playing a game on our computer and was excited because she had finally gotten to level 4. This level was, of course, more difficult than any of the preceding levels, and on her first attempt, she crashed and burned. On her second attempt, however, she maneuvered through the challenges with ease.

Later she told me that her stomach was in knots as she felt the pressure of playing at this harder level. *Then* she did something brilliant. On her second time through, she played a mental game with herself, telling herself she wasn't on level 4 after all, that she was really playing back on level 3. Suddenly her stomach relaxed, the pressure dissipated, and her performance improved.

I loved her strategy!

Sometimes, when I'm facing a challenge that feels like yesterday's problems on steroids, I take a deep, cleansing breath and try Kacie's strategy. I tell myself, "Hey, this isn't hard. I've been here before. I've beat this kind of thing before, and I'll do it again. Piece of cake, baby, piece of cake."

3. "Engage your C.O.R.E."

Stoltz and Weihenmayer encourage anyone facing adversity to dig in and take control. They admit, however, that this is easier said than done. Weihenmayer writes, "What do you do when some of the most important factors are completely out of your control, when the adversity is too big . . . or when the goal you set out to achieve appears genuinely impossible? . . . Most people back down or break. But there are a rare few who prevail and emerge stronger and better as a result. I've always been intrigued by the difference."[3]

What follows is a gripping story of Weihenmayer as he faced a particularly grueling stretch on his climb to the summit of Mount Everest. He spends two pages describing the treacheries of a hellish portion of the climb called the Icefall. (I'd like to go on record as saying that making ten trips across an icy chasm by crawling across five swaying aluminum ladders lashed together with nylon twine is not my idea of a good time.)

He writes,

> I knew there were many elements of the Icefall over which I had no influence, like the random collapses, the terrible terrain, and the immense distance; but there were many more things I could Control (C). I couldn't let my fate be determined by an outside force. I needed to take Ownership (O) of my own progress. I couldn't let

today's adversity Reach (R) into every other aspect of the climb or allow it to contaminate the outlook of the whole team. The Icefall was just one stage, and I had to contain it. Last, I couldn't sucker myself into imagining that today's nightmare would Endure (E) for the rest of the climb. Although it was a mental-wrestling-match, I had to see the Icefall as a puzzle that could be solved.[4]

Wow. The moment I read that paragraph, I recognized that these four principles have teeth and that, taken seriously, they can empower you and me to contain and master almost any adversity we may face. Engaging our C.O.R.E. is about taking charge of our thoughts and fears. It's a wartime strategy to win the battle that can wage in our minds when we face any bigger-than-life challenge.

- CONTROL the elements that you can control.
- Take OWNERSHIP of your own progress.
- Don't let this single adversity REACH into every part of your life and contaminate your outlook or relationships.
- Don't buy into the lie that today's nightmare will ENDURE forever.

The next time you face adversity, engage your C.O.R.E. In the meantime, if you find yourself swaying on an aluminum ladder suspended above an icy chasm, try to remember that other people have not only gone before you *and* lived to tell the story, they're making money on book sales and movie rights. Who knows? Maybe you can do the same!

4. "Waste not, want not."

At a divorce recovery workshop I heard a speaker describe what life was like in the wake of his divorce, then add through tears, "I don't want all this pain to have been for naught. I can't change the fact that it happened, but I can ask God to use this loss to change and refine me. I want to grow through this and past this. I don't want my divorce to have been in vain."

Later, in my small group, several people made references to this man's longing to emerge wiser and better rather than shriveled and bitter. Apparently his comments struck a chord in all of us.

It reminded me of a conversation I had years ago with the mother of a young man who had died of AIDS. When I asked her if I could write a book about her son's life, she said yes, adding, "It won't bring him back, but if someone else can be helped, at least his death won't have been in vain."

50. Pass the Elmer's.
Remember when you were in preschool and your favorite part of the day (besides the cookies) was craft time? The next time you spot a Nike magazine ad featuring the Just Do It slogan, tear it out (let's hope you own the magazine!) and arrange it on a bulletin board or poster board with pictures or illustrations that represent the changes you want to embrace in your life.
After that, have some milk and graham crackers, and take a nap with a fuzzy blanket. You'll be surprised how much better you feel.

A counselor I know told a struggling couple to take advantage of every fight they have. "Arguments don't feel good, but if done right, they can establish boundaries and bring our needs and fears into the light. They can be defining moments. Ask yourself, 'What did this show me about myself? How can we handle something like this differently in the future? Did we learn anything about how to embrace healthier boundaries? how to communicate more honestly? forgive? understand our individual needs or fears?'

"Learn from every encounter. Never, never, never let a good fight go to waste."

Sometimes we have control over circumstances that occur in our lives; sometimes we don't. But we always have control over how we respond and whether we grow bigger or bitter as a result of adversity.

Adversity isn't cheap. We pay a price emotionally, physically, spiritually, relationally, or even financially. Don't let the price you paid have been in vain.

5. "Come on in; the water's fine!"

Clayton is twenty and, in two months, will be moving from Colorado to Alaska to work on a fishing rig for a year. It's a tough job. I imagine fourteen months from now he'll have a lot to say about surviving and even thriving in the face of adversity. But if you ask me, he's got a good handle on the subject already.

He told me, "If you get caught out in the rain, you have two choices: You can curse the rain and do everything you can to avoid getting wet. But that's not going to happen, and you're only going to be miserable. Or you can embrace the rain, allow yourself to get wet, and enjoy it."

His words made me think of two very different images, the first of someone hurrying like a wet rat through the downpour, wearing a soggy newspaper on her head and a scowl on her face. The second was of someone dancing in the rain with outstretched arms and upturned face, laughing, tongue extended to taste the drops.

Even Weihenmayer and Stoltz point out the difference between a "Take it away!" attitude versus a "Take it on!" attitude. Stoltz writes, "Adversity happens. It doesn't play favorites, and it comes in all shapes and sizes. And your natural response might be 'Take it away!' rather than 'Take it on!'"[5] They describe five approaches to adversity, starting with avoidance, which they point out can be exhausting. After avoidance comes surviving, then coping, then managing. The best and most effective way to approach adversity is harnessing, which can leave you in a better place than before the adversity came along. "Adversity can sap your life force," Stoltz adds. "But it needn't do that. Why spend your best effort fighting the very wind that can fill your sails and take you to otherwise unreachable lands?"[6]

6. "Yoda knows best."

One time Skippy put it to me this way: "When it comes to rising above adversity, it's simple. You do it. You grit your teeth and plow forward, adapting as necessary, but moving forward and doing whatever you need to do to get to the other side. Like Yoda told Luke, 'Do. Or do not. There is no *try.*'"[7] If you ask me, Skippy and Yoda are on to something. In fact, this same person (Skippy, not Yoda) gave me the following advice when he discovered that I was feeling distraught over bills and parenting and housework and deadlines:

> Cowgirl up. Pay your bills on time, love your daughters, take care of your house, and do your job. And that's it. Suck it up, buttercup. I know you can do it. Sometimes I sugarcoat it with you; other times I don't sugarcoat it. You're a strong woman. C'mon. You're thirty-seven years old. I know you can handle it.

And you know what? After his tough-love approach, I actually felt better! (And no, I wasn't thirty-seven. He knew my age but always pretended he thought I was thirty-seven. See why I loved him?)

---

51. Read Psalm 57.

Talk about adversity! The composer of this ancient song describes calamities, lions, and hotheaded enemies with teeth like spears and arrows! Yet he finds mercy and refuge in the shadow of God's wings. I think my favorite line of all is found in verse 7, where David wrote, "My heart is steadfast, O God, my heart is steadfast."

Read this short psalm, and ask yourself how steadfast *you* feel in the heat of adversity. And if your answer is, "Not very," consider where David found mercy and refuge. Maybe you can find what you need there as well.

The whole thing makes me think of that Nike slogan, Just Do It. And how do we "just do it" when we encounter adversity?

- Remember that we are stronger, smarter, and better equipped than we've ever been before.

248

- Tell ourselves, "This is *such* a piece of cake!"
- Engage our C.O.R.E.
- Don't waste perfectly good adversity. (Remember, your current adversity has already taken a toll, so you might as well get something out if it in exchange for all that pain. Let it make you bigger, not bitter.)
- Stop trying to avoid or deny your adversity, and jump in and take it on, baby!
- When all else fails, picture Yoda wearing Nikes, reminding you to "Stop trying and just do it!"

It's tempting to wish that adversity would disappear from our lives, that there was a way to make obstacles obsolete, and that you and I would never have to experience hail dents and dings on the road of life.

Then again, without obstacles we wouldn't be stronger and smarter. And we definitely couldn't embrace any changes in our lives. In fact, if we give adversity permission to crush us, we might as well kiss transformation good-bye, because adversity and change go hand in hand. Sometimes adversity precedes change, sometimes it accompanies it, but like the right and left pedals on a bicycle, adversity and change work together to help us get to where we want to go.

Even if we *do* get there with hail dents on our hoods.

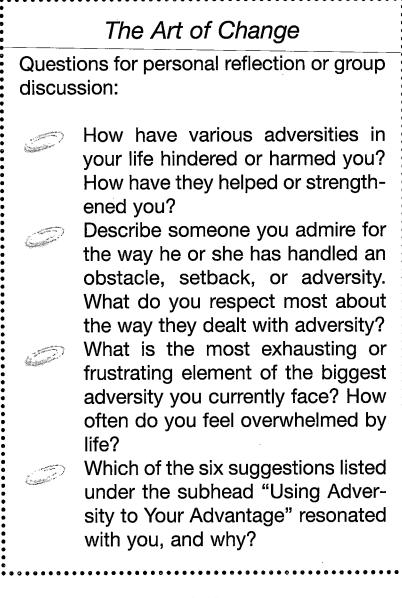

The Art of Change

Questions for personal reflection or group discussion:

- How have various adversities in your life hindered or harmed you? How have they helped or strengthened you?
- Describe someone you admire for the way he or she has handled an obstacle, setback, or adversity. What do you respect most about the way they dealt with adversity?
- What is the most exhausting or frustrating element of the biggest adversity you currently face? How often do you feel overwhelmed by life?
- Which of the six suggestions listed under the subhead "Using Adversity to Your Advantage" resonated with you, and why?

12

FEELING LISTLESS AND STUCK? POWER UP.

A JOURNEY OF A THOUSAND MILES BEGINS AT THE FUEL PUMP

Sitting in the historic City Auditorium, I glanced down the row of rickety wooden theater seats. In the row beside me were a couple of friends, Jieils and Jennifer, as well as most of my family, including my daughters, nephews, one sister, an aunt, and parents. Ranging in age from nine to seventy-five, we were an eclectic group. Below us, on the wooden floor of the eighty-year-old auditorium, women wearing jerseys and moving at high speeds were shoving and taunting each other.

We'd come to see the roller derby.

As soon as Jieils had told me the roller derby was coming to town, I'd gotten on the phone and rallied my family. After all, I had fond memories of watching the Pittsburgh Bombers in the early seventies on our little black-and-white television, on one of the five stations we could get back then. This was going to be *such* a blast from the past! The entire family agreed. My aunt Jeanette said yes in a heartbeat. Dad sprung for all our tickets. Even my mom — a classy woman who is an accomplished musician, is well read on politics and archaeology, and clucks her tongue whenever her grown daughters wear blue jeans to church — thought the evening sounded like fun.

But now, sweating in the un-air-conditioned auditorium with three generations in tow, I wasn't so sure. The athletes skating in circles below us seemed talented, but something was missing. Sure, it still smacked of the rowdy tactics and melodrama that were reminiscent of the seventies phenomenon, but it just didn't have the same zing.

Maybe it was the stifling heat inside the auditorium. Maybe it was the fact that the last time I'd really followed roller derby, I was eleven years old and pretty much *everything* in my world seemed exciting and larger than life. Maybe without an announcer adding hype and color, the action on the oval track was harder to follow. Whatever the reasons, when someone suggested we duck out early, it sounded like a good idea.

The auditorium was noisy, so I passed the

question — "Should we leave at halftime?" — telephone-style down the row. When it got to Dad, he looked relieved. My aunt flashed me a thumbs-up. Jieils and Jennifer had already bolted. Even the kids nodded their heads vigorously in agreement.

My mom was sitting at the very end of the row. I watched Kacie whisper the message in her ear. A moment later my phone beeped with an incoming text from Kacie.

"She says she wants to stay."

What?

Jostling past a lineup of kneecaps, I made my way to the nearest aisle, climbed a flight of stairs, walked behind our seating section, down another flight of stairs, and finally made it to the aisle seat where my mom was sitting. I figured she hadn't heard the question right. I squatted beside her.

"We were thinking of leaving at halftime," I yelled over the noise of the crowd. "Sound good to you?"

My mom's eyes danced with excitement, and there was a stubborn set to her dainty chin. She said decidedly, "I'm not going anywhere! Our team is behind, and we can't abandon them! They need us!"

No amount of cajoling could convince her otherwise. Dad shrugged. My aunt sighed. The kids groaned and dropped their heads into their hands. I texted Jieils, letting him know we were staying. He texted back, bidding us well and farewell. He and Jennifer were already blocks away.

The halftime show began with skating contests and T-shirt giveaways and ended with a performance by a live band.

Now, I *like* loud music. And this band was definitely loud. As far as their musical abilities . . . well, let's just say that even the teenagers around me had their hands over their ears. Sometimes brute energy isn't enough.

Four minutes into their performance I felt my phone vibrate. I looked at the screen and saw my mom's name. Then I peered down the row. Her seat and Dad's were empty.

I opened my phone. "Where *are* you?" I yelled over the din.

"We're in the car," my mom said cheerily. "Actually, we're just about to pull into the parking lot of the Chili's down the street. I couldn't stand that awful music one more second! Join us when you can!"

Our roller derby adventure taught me a lot of things. For example . . .

- Some childhood memories aren't the same when you try to relive them.

- Beneath Mom's pearls and cashmere beats the heart of a loyal sports fan.
- Finally, never underestimate the power of brute energy. Sometimes it's *exactly* what you need to get you moving quickly and efficiently from point A to point B.

Want Change? You're Going to Need Energy

Looking back through the pages of this book, I made a short list of some of the things we've talked about:

- dissatisfaction
- vision
- making decisions and sticking to them
- positive catalysts
- being aware of our habits
- upgrading our habits
- procrastination
- fear of failure
- the power of prayer
- letting go of whatever's holding us back
- rising above adversity and setbacks

No matter what changes you long to embrace, knowing how to manage and harness all of the above will serve you well. But there's one more thing I want you to know, and it's this: Change means getting from where you are to where you want to be, which means movement, and movement requires *energy.*

So where do we get all that energy? Being driven from an auditorium by a band mimicking a nuclear explosion works fine on special occasions, but for everyday use it seems a bit unwieldy. There's got to be another way.

WHAT MOVES YOU?

What kind of stuff fuels, moves, or motivates you to action? As far as I can tell, here are some energizing factors that apply to just about anyone.

Food, hydration, sleep, and exercise

You and I can have the best intentions in the world, but if we're too fat, weak, fatigued, or self-medicated on junk food to feel energetic, we're going to have a tougher time creating positive change in our lives. On the other hand, when our physical strength and energy are topnotch, that's a lot of oomph we can apply to pretty much anything we want to pursue. You want more energy? Taking a fresh look at how you eat, drink, sleep, and move is a great place to start.

Your thoughts

One day last summer I was jogging, moving along at a decent pace, feeling good, listening to music, and thinking pleasant thoughts. My energy level was good, and I figured I could go another ten minutes or more.

Then all of a sudden, a thought popped into my head. It was an unpleasant thought, something about lapsed insurance that I needed to resolve. *Immediately* my energy plummeted. I didn't have anything left. I stopped jogging and slowed to a heavy walk. I didn't make the connection at first — I just thought it was odd that I felt so tired when thirty seconds earlier I'd been really cruising.

When it happened again on a different day, I started to pay attention. I never *tried* to think unpleasant, negative thoughts on purpose. But whenever my energy suddenly dropped and I found myself overcome with fatigue, I examined my thoughts and realized, yep, a thought had just crossed my mind about something unpleasant, perhaps an unresolved conflict or health concern or worry about one of my kids.

How does this work? I'm not entirely sure, but the fact that bodies respond to thought is hardly news. Think, *My nose itches,* and suddenly you're scratching your nose. Think,

Look at the time! The eBay auction is about to end! and the next thing you know you're frantically typing in your password and clicking on the link to raise your bid. We think; our bodies respond. So can sad thoughts make us tired? A mental health article from the University of New Mexico asserts that they can, explaining that disappointment, sadness, or negative thoughts can trigger sensations of weakness, fatigue, or even unexplained pain.[1]

Even our memories may have more of a direct impact on our bodies than we realized. Many scientists believe memories aren't stored just in our brains but also throughout our bodies, including our nervous system and even muscles. The connection between our emotions, thoughts, and bodies is still vastly unexplored. It'll be interesting to see what mysteries are explained in years to come regarding the intimate link between our thoughts and bodies!

Your words

Words are another form of energy. At their most basic level, even without the meaning of language attached to them, spoken words are sound waves. It's no secret that sound waves can leave things changed in their wake. Think of the high-pitched note that breaks a glass, the gunshot that sets off an avalanche, the sound wave known as ultrasound that can pulverize a kidney stone.

How extensive is the link between sound, vibrations, and physical reality? By passing sound waves through sand, Swiss scientist Hans Jenny proved that every sound creates its own distinct, consistent pattern. Some sounds create beautiful, orderly patterns while other sounds create chaotic, broken patterns. Other scientists have discovered the same phenomenon: When freezing water is exposed to classical music or gentle words, the ice crystals that form are delicate and orderly. Rock music or harsh words create ice crystals that are broken and in disarray.

If certain sounds and words create orderly patterns in sand and ice, could the right sounds or words influence or even repair genes, cells, and other structures in the body? It's fascinating to ponder, don't you think? And sound waves are only one of the reasons our words create impact. After all, our words not only create vibrations, they also convey meaning, shaping our thoughts, emotions, and interpretations of everything that happens to us.

Your relationships

Whether we're in a relationship with one

person or with a community of people, relationships move us. When we enjoy intimate connection with other people and share parts of our lives, there's a synergy that takes place. We grow and change. Relationships bring out the best — and sometimes the worst — in us. Relationships have an energy all their own. They can drive us to become a better version of ourselves. They can also entice us to become a baser version of ourselves. The thing that a close relationship will never do is leave us unchanged.

How are you being changed and molded by your current relationships? Are they moving you in directions you want to go?

Things that take on lives of their own

Money isn't organic. It doesn't generate energy or synergy in the same way that our bodies, thoughts, words, and relationships do. But money — or more precisely, the way we handle money — can take on a life and momentum of its own. Spending seems to lead to more spending, while earning and saving encourage more of the same. Investments can take on a life of their own too, accumulating profits while we do nothing.

Any of your habits can do the same thing. A TV-watching habit can take on a life of its own. Positive habits such as serving others or working out can take on lives of their own as well. And addictions — habits on steroids, really — *definitely* take on lives of their own, gathering momentum until they are driving most of our choices and our needs. Think about the situations you've experienced or heard about where addictions to things like pornography, gambling, affairs, alcohol, or drugs have destroyed marriages and even lives.

Your emotions

What emotions do we nurse and rehearse? Lust? Grudges? Kindness? Forgiveness? Faith? Hopelessness? Anxiety? Peace? Love? The energy that is created by each emotion is distinct from the others. It's normal to experience all of these emotions. But depending on which emotions we embrace and nurture as our favorites, we can generate momentum that will propel us either down a path we love or a path we'll regret.

For example, it's common sense that if we are intentional about cultivating emotions such as peace, love, kindness, and forgiveness, our lives and relationships will be impacted. Likewise, if we allow ourselves to gravitate toward anxiety, hopelessness, anger, unforgiveness, selfishness, and the like, we may find our lives and relationships

261

have taken a turn we don't want.

Your energy

A steady diet of ice cream and sugary cereal might give us a temporary high, but it's not going to provide the kind of steady, stable energy we can count on. Likewise, the stuff we shovel into our minds and spirits will generate energy too. But what *kind* of energy? If we feast our senses on pornography, there's a good chance we'll create desires and energy that will move us down paths we'll later regret.

When it comes to the things we look at, read, watch, listen to, and think about, what exactly are we feeding on? And more importantly, what quality of energy are they producing in our lives?

NO ENERGY CRISIS HERE! SO WHY AM I STILL STUCK?

There is a lot of energy available to us. And I haven't even identified all of the elements we can use as motivation to get off our rumps and get moving toward the changes we long to embrace. So why are we still stuck?

I've decided it has to do with dogs. No, really. I'm serious. It's dogs. Sled dogs, to be exact.

Imagine something with me for a moment. This will help us both get a better grasp on why in the world — with all that raw energy at our disposal — we're still parked at a green light, in neutral, with our engines idling. If you and I can really understand the picture I'm about to paint, I'm convinced we can generate exactly what we need to bear down hard on our wildest dreams, whatever they may be.

Picture yourself stranded on a dogsled somewhere in the winter wilds of Alaska. You are surrounded by expanses of frigid, frozen, snowy terrain, when where you *really* want to be is twenty miles away with all your friends in the cozy lodge in town. It's not like you don't have dogs. You've actually got really *big* dogs. But for some reason you're not moving and you can't figure out why.

Surveying your team of dogs, you notice that Juno over there is scratching at fleas.

Spot is straining at his harness, wanting to chase a passing caribou.

Cody and Max have escaped their harnesses and are tussling and growling and wrestling in the snow.

Samson snuck onto the back of the sled and is curled up fast asleep.

Sasha is chasing her tail.

With all these pooches, you've got plenty

of power. But until you get them harnessed *and* pulling in the same direction, you're not going anywhere. Even if you can get two or three dogs pulling in the same direction, as long as the others are tugging in other directions, you're not going to make the progress you long for.

What you need is brute energy — and plenty of it — *harnessed and propelling you in a single direction.* And if you can't make that happen, well, break out the parka, baby, because you're in for a long, cold night.

52. Train them dogs.

Talk about adversity! Identify one of the changes you'd love to make; then ask yourself what "dogs" are propelling you forward and which ones are pulling you in the wrong direction.

Here's where I want to get to:

Good doggies:

Bad doggies:

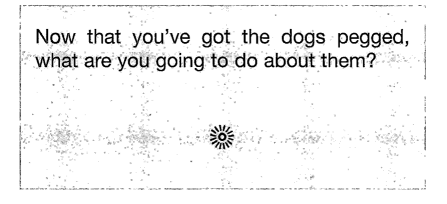

Now that you've got the dogs pegged, what are you going to do about them?

TIME FOR A TASTY ILLUSTRATION

My friend Ilene stood inside my pantry and shook her head. And when I say she stood inside my pantry, I'm not exaggerating. My pantry is the size of an office complex. The other day my ten-year-old nephew, Isaac, was over. I was loading the dishwasher as he and Kacie walked past me, opened the pantry door, stepped inside, and closed the door behind them. I heard chairs scraping the floor and then the rattle of cellophane.

A few minutes later, my sister arrived to pick up her son. Walking into the kitchen, she said, "Where's Isaac?"

"In the boardroom."

She looked at the closed pantry door. "Again? Why do they always hang out in there?"

I shrugged and put another dish away. "Oh, you know. The usual. Plotting against terrorists. Visualizing world peace. Sneaking marshmallows and canned frosting."

But I digress.

As I was saying, Ilene was standing in my very large pantry shaking her head. "This place is a binge waiting to happen," she said. "How can you even *think* about staying on your diet with all this junk food in here?"

"I *think* about it just fine," I said. "Although, now that you mention it, *doing* does pose a bit of a problem . . ."

Ilene had a good point.

When it came to reaching my weight-loss destination, I had a few good sled dogs — exercise, hydration, and attitude — pulling me in the right direction. After all, I not only went walking every day and drank plenty of water, I'd taped pieces of paper shouting motivational sayings all over my kitchen.

Still, every night I'd hear tempting foods call my name (and I usually answered). Regularly skimping on sleep wasn't helping either, leaving me with more appetite and less willpower the following day. In other words, with a few dogs straining to pull me forward and a couple more straining to hold their ground, no wonder I wasn't getting where I longed to be!

Mush, baby, mush!

If you want to get someplace other than where you are, and you want to get there

with speed and efficiency, *train your dogs!*
Harness:

- how you use your body
- what goes on in your thoughts
- what comes out of your mouth
- the caliber of your relationships
- how you spend your time
- how you manage your finances
- what goes on in your emotions
- how you feed your spirit

. . . and get everything heading in the same direction!

If each of these things were a sled dog, would you want it running around independent of the rest of the team, pulling in its own direction, canceling out the other dogs and undoing your forward momentum? Or would you want every canine working hard for you, harnessed and unified, pulling you smartly in the direction you want to go?

Whatever change you long to make, are you harnessing all your energies in the same direction, or are you letting valuable muscle go to waste?

And after all that, if you *still* can't budge and you need something *really* drastic to get you up and running, call my mom. If you're in luck, she just might remember the name of that band. After all, they *did* move us on out of that roller derby exhibition before we got so desperate we chewed off a paw.

The Art of Change

Questions for personal reflection or group discussion:

Is an energy crisis stopping you from changing your life? Are you experiencing physical fatigue or mental/ emotional fatigue or both? Sometimes they feed each other, but sometimes it's possible to distinguish between the two. Can you?

It's possible you have plenty of energy, but it's not taking you in a helpful direction. Is there something in your life — a relationship, habit, addiction, or obsession — that is propelling you down a side street or maybe even a dark alley? If so, how does this impact your motivation to pursue the healthy changes you say you'd like to make?

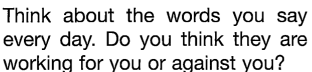

Think about the words you say every day. Do you think they are working for you or against you?

Are you taking care of your health? What are you doing (or not doing) that could be keeping you from feeling as lively and energetic as you'd like? If you were limited to making just one change related to your health and fitness, what would it be?

Identify one small, easy change you could make this week that could increase your energy level. (How 'bout drinking more water? cutting back on coffee? going to bed half an hour earlier? taking your dog outside for a real walk instead of leashing him to your treadmill like you usually do?)

EPILOGUE

HUMOR REQUIRED.
SANITY OPTIONAL.

Life is crazy, isn't it? We plan and dream and strive . . . and then life hands us something we didn't expect. Sometimes the surprises are pleasant; sometimes they make us groan. If you ask me, life isn't like a box of chocolates as much as a box of Cracker Jack with you and me as the nuts.

When it comes to life, anything can happen. And usually does. With conditions like these, how do we hang on to our sanity? Or maybe the real question is, should we even try?

Isn't it *great?*

I love life. And the fact that you've hung with me this far makes me think that you do too. Sure, you and I want to make big plans, visualize change, pursue our passions. We want to get out of life the things we dream about. But it's also okay to love what we get. And the two don't always match.

I guess what I'm saying is this: I'm all about change. Transformation, improvements, and growth are good things. Very good things. But as we strive for more, let's not forget to enjoy what we have. Today. As is. With no strings, regrets, or blueprints attached.

You and I started this book with the question, "What kinds of changes have you been longing to make?" We agreed to identify principles that could apply to pretty much any healthy, positive change we might yearn to embrace. Since then, we've learned how to harness things like dissatisfaction, imagination, decisions, catalysts, habits, and even adversity. We've figured out how to overcome procrastination and fear of failure, and how to jettison the excess baggage that slows us down. Finally, we've learned a few things about synergy and how to corral our energies into working together to pull us toward a single goal.

Having done all that, there's one thing left to do: *enjoy the ride.*

How do we do that? I think we do it by laughing, learning, and loving — and above all, hoping and believing.

A friend of mine is going through a tough time. She called me the other night, feeling anxious and scared. I told her, "Everything's going to be all right. *You're* going to be all right."

"Really?" At that moment, she sounded like a fearful seven-year-old in need of re-assurance. "You promise?"

"I promise."

She let out a raggedy sigh. "Thank you," she said. "I needed to hear that. Whether or not it's true, I really needed to hear it."

I believe it *is* true. I believe it for her. I believe it for me. And I believe it for you.

We *can* embrace the changes we yearn for. But in the meantime, if change takes longer than we thought, if life throws us a curve ball, if our priorities shift midstream, we're going to be okay. Even if we lose our job or our house, our temper or our spouse, only two measly pounds instead of twenty, our hair, our health, or even just the keys to the car — again! — it's going to be all right. We'll figure it out. We're going to be okay.

Sound impossible? Of course it does!

And your point would be . . . what?

I love the following exchange from *Alice's Adventures in Wonderland.* I think you're going to love it too.

"I can't believe that!" said Alice.

"Can't you?" the Queen said in a pitying tone. "Try again: draw a long breath, and shut your eyes."

Alice laughed. "There's no use trying," she said. "One *can't* believe impossible things."

"I dare say you haven't had much practice," said the Queen. "When I was your age, I always did it for half-an-hour a day. Why, sometimes I've believed as many as six impossible things before breakfast."[1]

Go ahead, believe the impossible. After all, anything can happen, remember? There are surprises around the corner. Good ones. I promise.

And speaking of surprises . . .

I spoke with Skippy not long ago. It started with a text message, then a phone call, and a few days later we saw each other for the first time in about a year and a half. The visit felt very healing. Turns out he'd hurt over me as much as I'd hurt over him. We didn't exchange a barrage of details or explanations. Instead, we held each other and said, "I'm sorry."

He broke the news that his company was transferring him to a new office and he would be moving in two weeks.

I broke the news that I'd referred to him in my last book — and that I'd named him Skippy.

He laughed. "Skippy? You named me *Skippy?*"

"Are you upset?"

"No. I knew you'd write about it at some point. It's what you do, how you make sense of life. You couldn't *not* write about stuff even if you tried. It's one of the things I love about you. And who knows? Maybe one day you'll write a book and call it *I Married Skippy.*"

Isn't life wild? We never know what's around the corner, do we? But even with all the mystery and the unknowns, here's something that I know for sure: You and I are never stuck, or stagnant, or without hope. We're not powerless. We may not get everything we want, but there's usually something we yearn for hidden inside whatever we do get. And no matter what we've experienced or how many disappointments we've had, we're never quite out of surprises and even miracles.

Get ready. Be encouraged. Change is in the air!

NOTES

Chapter 1

1. Society for Neuroscience, Brain Briefings, "Sleep Deficits," Summer 2007, www.sfn.org/index.cfm?pagename =brainBriefings _sleepdeficits.

Chapter 2

1. Vincent van Gogh, *Letters to an Artist: From Vincent van Gogh to Anton Ridder van Rappard, 1881–1885* (New York: Viking, 1936), 107.
2. Henry David Thoreau, *Walden* (London: J. M. Dent/Orion, 1995), 255.
3. Matthew Kelly, *The Rhythm of Life: Living Every Day with Passion and Purpose,* new ed. (New York: Fireside, 2004), 32.

Chapter 4

1. Kelly, *Rhythm of Life,* 62.

Chapter 5

1. Kelly, *Rhythm of Life,* 115.

Chapter 6
1. The three Ds are adapted from Brian Tracy, *Eat That Frog! Twenty-One Great Ways to Stop Procrastinating and Get More Done in Less Time* (San Francisco: Berrett-Koehler, 2007), 6.

Chapter 7
1. Kevin P. Austin, "Procrastination," Caltech Counseling Center, www.counseling.caltech.edu/articles/procrastination.html.
2. Brian Tracy, *Eat That Frog!* 4–5.

Chapter 8
1. Ralph Waldo Emerson, quoted in David Allen, *Ready for Anything* (London: Penguin, 2003), 24.

Chapter 10
1. Viktor Frankl, *Man's Search for Meaning* (Boston: Beacon, 1959), 148.
2. Chris Gardner, *The Pursuit of Happyness* (New York: HarperCollins, 2006), 247.
3. Kelly, *Rhythm of Life,* 4.
4. Kelly, *Rhythm of Life,* 4.
5. Author's paraphrase of Hebrews 11:1.

6. Ernest Hemingway, *A Moveable Feast* (New York: Simon & Schuster, 1964), 12.

Chapter 11

1. Paul G. Stoltz and Erik Weihenmayer, *The Adversity Advantage: Turning Everyday Struggles into Everyday Greatness* (New York: Fireside, 2006), 1.

2. Gordon Stewart, quoted in Maria Bartiromo, "Dreamers: King of Vacations," *Reader's Digest,* January 2008, www.rd.com/hard-work-pays-off-for-butch-stewart/article50635.html/.

3. Stoltz and Weihenmayer, *Adversity Advantage,* 98.

4. Stoltz and Weihenmayer, *Adversity Advantage,* 98.

5. Stoltz and Weihenmayer, *Adversity Advantage,* 26.

6. Stoltz and Weihenmayer, *Adversity Advantage,* 26.

7. *The Empire Strikes Back,* DVD, directed by Irvin Kershner (1980; Beverly Hills, CA: Twentieth Century Fox Home Entertainment, 2004).

Chapter 12

1. University of New Mexico, "CARS [Counseling, Assistance and Referral

Services] Presents . . . Mindfulness Based Cognitive Therapy (MBCT)," January 2003, www.unm.edu/~hrinfo/pages/MBCT .pdf.

Epilogue

1. Lewis Carroll, *Alice's Adventures in Wonderland and Through the Looking Glass* (New York: Signet Classics/Penguin, 1960), 176.

ABOUT THE AUTHOR

A motivational speaker, inspirational speaker, and author of ten humorous self-help books, **Karen Linamen** mixes up a potent blend of laugh-out-loud humor and sage advice. Whether addressing audiences from page or platform, Karen is entertaining, passionate, and transparent as she encourages people toward wellness in their relationships, emotions, bodies, and spirits. Her enthusiastic theme is "Yes. You can." And she preaches it passionately whether she's talking about embracing change, pursuing dreams, forgiving, making healthier choices, handling stress, or living and laughing more boldly than ever before.

To book Karen as a speaker for your church, corporate, or community event, visit her at www.karenlinamen.com.

Karen lives in Colorado Springs, Colorado.